¶ The author is Professor of Arabic at the
University of Edinburgh.

ISLAMIC REVELATION

ISLAMIC REVELATION IN THE MODERN WORLD

W. MONTGOMERY WATT

EDINBURGH
at the University Press

© W. Montgomery Watt, 1969
EDINBURGH UNIVERSITY PRESS
22 George Square, Edinburgh
85224 166 6
North America
Aldine Publishing Company
529 South Wabash Avenue, Chicago
Library of Congress
Catalog Card Number 70-103615
Printed in Great Britain by
T. & A. Constable Ltd, Edinburgh

PREFACE

This book, unlike my other works on Islam, is not purely academic, but has a large personal element, for it is an attempt to state the position I have reached after over thirty years' reflection on the relationship of Islam and Christianity. Some personal details will thus not be out of place.

My interest in Islam began with a personal contact. In the autumn of 1937 a veterinary student from Lahore came to share my flat for six or eight months. He belonged to the Qadiani Ahmadiyya and was rather argumentative; and the arguments which began over the supper-table aroused my interest in the religion of Islam. Thus in a sense my contact with Islam began with dialogue. I had the impression, too, that I was confronting not just this individual, but a whole centuries-old system of thought. This glimpse of the profundity of the problem of the relationships of Christianity and Islam fascinated me. I happened to be at a turning-point in my career where a fresh initiative was necessary in any case. So I made a decision and set about preparations which eventually led to me spending nearly three years in Jerusalem (then under British mandate) as an Arabic and Islamic specialist on the staff of the Anglican bishop there. From that appointment events produced an easy transition to the academic work which has occupied me since 1947, namely, lecturing on Arabic language and literature and researching on various aspects of Islam as a religion.

There is something paradoxical in thus being immersed in an alien religion. The situation causes tensions in one's inner being which have somehow or other to be resolved. In my own case the resolution of the tension seems to have come about through moving on to a new, deeper or higher, level (as suggested on p. 125) where I am, as it were, intellectually detached from both religions, while continuing to practise one. Stages in this advance to a new level are indicated by my

v

books, *The Reality of God* (1957), *The Cure for Human Troubles* (1959), and *Truth in the Religions* (1963), as well as by passages in other books and articles. The present book carries the same line of thought further, though it speaks mainly, not about Christianity nor religion in general, but about Islam.

The genesis of this essay may be traced back to the publication of L. S. Thornton's *Revelation in the Modern World* in 1950. I reviewed this in the *Philosophical Quarterly* (iii. 90f.), and also planned to write an article applying Thornton's ideas to Islam. The article, in fact, was never written; and in part its place was taken by the books mentioned above. After the appearance of the last of these, however, it occurred to me in the continuing process of reflection that I might write something about Islamic revelation using Thornton's conceptions as a framework. The plan gradually took shape. It was worked out in detail during a visit to Makerere University College, Uganda, in 1967, and written rapidly in the months following my return. I am very grateful to Professor Noel King (now of the University of California, Santa Cruz) and to his colleagues in the Department of Religious Studies, Makerere, for providing such a congenial atmosphere for work. The title I have chosen attempts to acknowledge my indebtedness to Lionel Thornton's book.

My primary aim in this essay is, consonantly with sound scholarship, to present Islam in the best light possible to European and American readers, both the religiously-minded and the secular in outlook. In part this is intended to counteract the residual effects of medieval war-propaganda, but even more it is an attempt to bring about a fuller realization of the importance Islam is likely to have in the next hundred years. A secondary aim is to show Muslims that the attitudes of occidental scholarship are not necessarily hostile to Islam as a religion but that it is possible to combine these attitudes with a loyal, though more sophisticated, acceptance of it.

As I was writing this Preface there came into my hands Willem A. Bijlefeld's Inaugural Lecture as Professor of Islamics at Hartford Seminary (*Muslim World*, lix. 1–28). In the course of this he points out that my attempt (in *Muhammad Prophet and Statesman*, 237f.) to answer the question 'Was Muḥammad a prophet?' goes beyond the discipline of 'history of religions', and he seems to suggest that we cannot respond 'to the Qur'anic appeal to believe in and to obey God and His Prophet-Apostle' except on the basis of a Qur'anic concept of prophethood (pp. 7f.). My distinction above between academic and personal is roughly in line with his first point, but I must disagree firmly with his second. Dialogue, as I see it, involves a readiness to respond positively (that is, with some degree of acceptance) to the assertions of the other religion yet without transferring one's allegiance to it. Without some readiness to learn on both sides dialogue is a kind of concealed proselytizing. This book attempts to give a justification of open dialogue of this type, and in so doing necessarily (I would say) moves away from the official formulations of both religious communities.

I hope this explanation of the origins of the book will enable the reader to appreciate more fully what it is trying to do.

W. Montgomery Watt
Edinburgh, August 1969

NOTE

The Qur'anic references are to the verse numbers in the official Egyptian text, followed (after a diagonal) by the Flügel verse number where the two differ. The index gives only the Egyptian numbering.

THE CONTENTS

CONTENTS

ONE

THE APPROACH

༄

1. The Problems

One of the great facts about the later twentieth century is that the world has become an 'inter-religious' world. Especially since the Second World War the adherents of different religions have been mixing with one another on a scale unprecedented in world history. There was something like it in the Roman Empire during the first three Christian centuries. Within the framework provided by the imperial institutions of Rome various new religions were struggling for mastery. The old religions had not developed sufficiently rapidly to give men the support they needed to deal with the tensions produced by urbanized imperial life, and new religions began to fill the vacuum. That 'inter-religious' struggle, in which Christianity was eventually successful, was on a much smaller scale than the 'inter-religious' encounter of today. For many centuries, until the impact of Europe began to be felt by non-European civilizations, each of the great religious and cultural units of the world lived its own life in almost complete isolation from the others. Stages in the breaking down of isolation were the discovery of the sea route to India by Vasco da Gama in 1498 and, especially for the Islamic Middle East, the invasion of Egypt by Napoleon in 1798. Since then the development of European technology and the greater ease and rapidity of communications have unified the world at the material level, while most parts of the world are now independent members of that European-type institution, the United Nations. This is the framework within which the encounter of world religions is taking place.

The implications of this great fact are only slowly being realized. One implication is that something like a Copernican revolution is required in our thinking – from being Europe-centred to being world-centred. For long, in all spheres, European civilization (and Christendom) has behaved as if it was the only section of mankind that mattered. (In the present context it seems justifiable to regard North American culture as an extension of European, though in other contexts it probably should be regarded as something distinct.) In the nineteenth century European culture *was* civilization, and as Europe expanded technologically and politically, other parts of the world became 'civilized'. World history was the history of the expansion of 'civilization', that is, in effect, of Europe; and the history of the great civilizations of the world before their contact with Europe was virtually neglected.

The religions of the world were treated in a similar way. The essential religious development of mankind was the Christian, though a small place was given to Judaism. What was beyond that was thought to be crude and primitive little better than the religions of the peoples on the border of Palestine which were so vehemently denounced by the prophets of the Old Testament. Just as these had disappeared and the Jewish religion alone been left, and just as the 'emotional' and 'irrational' religions of the Roman Empire had faded away or been absorbed by Christianity, so it was supposed that the other religions, even the great world religions, would quickly be superseded by Christianity.

The middle decades of the twentieth century have seen revolutionary changes in these attitudes, at least among the leaders of thought. Politically non-Europeans have been accepted as the equals of Europeans, and the United Nations have had an Asian secretary general. World history is now seen to include the rise and fall of empires and civilizations in complete isolation from Europe. Less clearly in the religious field it is being realized that religions other than the Christian have had memorable spiritual achievements in the past; and advanced Christian theologians are now saying that the adherents of these religions today must normally seek salvation within their own religious tradition. Some such admission is implicit in the conception of 'dialogue' which is now popular, for this means meeting adherents of other faiths as equals; but, if one genuinely meets them as equals, one's act has vast theological implications.

The encounter of religions, however, is not just a matter of

2

theory, but leads to problems at the practical level. The English vicar or Scottish minister may find that some of his flock have Pakistani Muslims as neighbours, and also that they consider them very decent people, not unlike themselves. He has therefore to help them towards a new conception of the relation of Christianity to other religions. The Christian parishioners have probably inherited the idea that all non-Christians were little better than primitive savages, and their world begins to fall in pieces around them when they discover that non-Christians can live decent civilized lives, be deeply concerned for the welfare of their children, and give as rational a justification of their beliefs as the Christians can of theirs. In such ways the great fact of the 'inter-religious' world is going increasingly to affect our daily lives. It is not only selected theologians but many ordinary Christians who are going to meet non-Christians in the workaday world, who will have to learn to treat them as equals, and who will sooner or later want guidance on the intellectual implications of what they are doing.

The 'inter-religious' problems are complicated by another great fact of this century, namely, the growth of what we may call the scientific outlook. By this is meant the modern mentality based on the achievements of science and accepting its methods as applicable to many spheres. Some people tend to go beyond the scientific outlook and to treat science as a kind of religion, capable of giving man answers to all his deepest questions; but this is something more than the scientific outlook as understood here. It has to be admitted, of course, that the scientific outlook cannot be linked with any definite intellectual system, tidy and complete, since there are differences between the various exponents of the scientific outlook, even if there is also much that they have in common. The position to be adopted in this study is that we must accept the assured results of science and also many of its probable hypotheses, and that we must accept the validity of scientific methods in most spheres of life, the chief exception being the sphere of values. To accept the omnicompetence of scientific method leads to a secular view of the world which has no place for religious and moral values. Many Christians now accept much of this secular view of the world and retain certain religious beliefs in uneasy juxtaposition with it. This difficulty in varying forms and degrees is felt by the adherents of all religions.

One of the basic convictions underlying this study is that the various cultural regions of the world, which were isolated from one another until recently, differ radically from one another in intellectual outlook. This is much more than a difference of belief. In each cultural region – and a cultural region is here taken to be roughly identical with the habitat of one of the great religions – formulated beliefs presuppose a whole system of thought, and this system of thought has been elaborated on the basis of a set of categories which are used in the analysis of human experience. Since these categories may differ fundamentally from region to region, it is difficult, and indeed at the moment impossible, to compare credal formulations in any meaningful way. This may be illustrated by considering certain Christian and Muslim expressions. Thus the phrase 'the will of God' is linguistically equivalent to *mashī'at Allāh* or *irādat Allāh*, but the relation of the phrases to the religious life of the Christian and the Muslim respectively is altogether different; for the Christian 'the will of God' usually means his moral will as expressed in commandments or in individual intuitions ('the will of God for me' in regard, say, to a job), whereas for the Muslim all that happens, happens by the will of God. Again 'religion' and *dīn* are linguistically equivalent, but for the Muslim religion covers nearly the whole of life, whereas for the average European Christian it is a very small part of it. Where there is no easy comparison, there can be no simple criterion of truth and falsehood.

Now if in the English or Scottish urban scene the nominally Christian John Smith begins to talk on religious subjects with his Pakistani neighbour, Muḥammad Aḥmad, they will quickly reach an impasse, for they will find that they are using the same words with different meanings. Since they have neither sufficient time, philosophical training nor interest to dig deeper, they will probably agree to differ. Should they decide to continue their discussions, however, they may find that their common attachment to the scientific outlook, while in some ways complicating their problems, occasionally makes communication easier. Each is trying to link up his religion with his version of the scientific world-view, and while this produces difficulties for each, it also affords some common ground. Both are immersed in the material culture of the modern world, of which the scientific outlook is the intellectual reflection. On the level of the scientific and secular world-view – if they have sufficient confidence in their personal solution of the difficulties – they may begin to communicate with one another.

The present study attempts to deal with only one aspect of the interreligious problem, namely, the relations of Christianity and Islam; and it further narrows this aspect by considering only the Islamic conception of revelation and matters closely associated with it. Part of the aim is to show Christians not yet aware of the point that the Islamic revelation must be taken seriously, that – in so far as it is legitimate to think in strategic terms – Islam is a dangerous rival of Christianity in the struggle for world leadership. It must be realized that much of our fathers' belief in the superiority of Christianity was a belief in the superiority of European material culture, and that simply as religions Christianity and Islam are roughly on an equal footing, that is to say, that Islam, just as much as Christianity, has a 'gospel' for the modern world.

The method of this study, however, is not a direct comparison of Islamic and Christian thought, but an attempt to relate both to the secular or rather neutral world-view associated with the scientific outlook. This world-view is secular in so far as it omits the religious aspect, but its secularity is not taken to include hostility to religion, and therefore it is perhaps better described as neutral. In this respect the study may be of some use to those in both religions who are struggling with the tensions between the religious and scientific outlooks.

2. A Preliminary Consideration of Revelation

According to the beliefs of Muslims the Qur'an is a revealed book or scripture. For them this further means that the Qur'an is the speech of God communicated to Muhammad by an angel. It is not in any way Muhammad's speech or the product of his mind, but the speech of God alone, addressed to Muhammad and his contemporaries, and conveyed to Muhammad by supernatural means. Muhammad was no more than the messenger chosen by God to carry the message. The message was directed in the first place to the people of Mecca, and then more generally to all the Arabs, and thus it takes the form of 'an Arabic Qur'an'. Yet there are a few verses in the Qur'an which indicate that it is even more widely relevant and has a message for the whole of mankind. This universal relevance is indeed confirmed by the world-wide spread of Islam and its acceptance by men of nearly every race.

Many Christians throughout the centuries have held a similar view of revelation, taking the words of the Bible to be the words of God himself. They have not usually supposed that the words were brought, externally as it were, by an angel to the writers of the sacred books, but they held that these writers were inspired in such a way that the words they wrote were in fact the words of God. The prophets of the Old Testament who unhesitatingly proclaimed 'Thus saith the Lord ...' must have believed that the words they spoke were in some sense truly the speech of God. The Bible, as a whole is called 'the word of God'. This conception of revelation, however, is modified by the fact that Christians regard the life and activity of Jesus as revelatory. Indeed, Jesus is also called 'the word of God'. Where this point of view is given weight, the previous conception of revelation is felt to be verbal and mechanical, and is partly abandoned.

The main trend in recent Christian thought is to regard revelation as an activity of God. In revelation God is revealing himself, and therefore revelation even when it has the form of language, has to be understood as God's act.[1] Another way of expressing this is to say that revelation has to be conceived as 'a mode of divine activity by which the Creator communicates himself to man and, by so doing, evokes man's response and cooperation.'[2] In so far as some such view is accepted, the older view that revelation 'is a deposit of truth laid up in scripture'[3] is seen to be inadequate, that is, not false, but in need of being supplemented. As against the lifeless and abstract character of the written word in isolation, revelation is seen to be an activity of God directed towards human beings and expecting a response from them. Thus it is embedded in the texture of life.

This conception of revelation as divine activity is not foreign to Islam, though it has received no emphasis from Muslim theologians. It may be said to be contained implicitly in the traditional Islamic view, since according to this view God chose Muhammad at a particular time to convey a message in the first place to the people of Mecca, just as he had previously chosen many other prophets and sent them to other peoples. God is active in choosing Muhammad and conveying the messages to him; and the messages are directed towards human beings. In course of time, Muhammad's function became more than that of a 'warner' or conveyer of messages; as a messenger of God and prophet he had in some ways to direct the affairs of the community of believers, and this also might be regarded as a form of God's activity. Whether that be admitted or not, a response from men was certainly envisaged. In the later parts of the Qur'an there are instructions and commands to guide the continuing response of the community. Thus the words quoted above of Christianity could be used exactly of Islamic revelation – it is 'a mode of divine activity by which the Creator communicates himself to man and, by so doing, evokes man's response and cooperation.' The one term which might give a Muslim pause is 'communicates himself'; but reflection should remove the difficulty here, for the Islamic insistence that the Qur'an is not created but is the uncreated speech of God is a way of saying that it expresses something of himself, of his inner being; and it is this that is communicated to men.

This way of regarding the matter should bring Muslims to look on the Qur'an not as something isolated, but as part of a wider whole embracing both the divine initiative and the human response. Strictly speaking, according to Islamic theology, the human response is at the same time a mode of divine activity, since it is 'created' by God and only 'acquired' or 'appropriated' by man – it is God's 'creation' (*khalq*) and man's 'acquisition' (*kasb*). Yet this way of interpreting the human response does not falsify the assertion that the divine initiative (in the Qur'an) and the human response together in some sense form a whole, in which the Qur'an has a special function. One can hardly say that the Qur'an is the instrument of the divine initiative, for it is God's speech, and speech is not exactly an instrument. One might say that it was the 'external' form or the 'embodiment' of the divine initiative.

It seems desirable at this point to say something about the

personal position of the writer with regard to the matters discussed, since they are such that complete neutrality and objectivity are hardly possible. I would say, then, that I hold the Qur'an to be in some sense the product of a divine initiative and therefore revelation. The qualifications indicated by the words 'in some sense' will become clear, I hope, in the course of my argument. This position – so far as I, an amateur in Christian theology, can tell – is in accordance with some of the most recent trends in Christian thought, especially among Roman Catholic theologians.[4] It is far removed, however, from the traditional Christian standpoint, and some readers may have difficulty in seeing how it can be accommodated to that standpoint. The difficulties should become less as Christians move towards a more secular and scientific outlook, and in particular as they adopt the sociological conceptions to be expounded in the next section, and are able to regard Christendom as 'the historical organism of Christianity' and to recognize it as an entity of the same type as 'the historical organism of Islam'. In so far, too, as Christians are in dialogue with antireligious secularists, they will find it impossible to maintain the claims of the Christian revelation without admitting some validity to the Islamic revelation.

The method I am adopting in this study is to proceed as far as possible at the purely factual level, and only in the closing chapters to look at the theoretical theological questions. This means that the assertions of Muslims about the Qur'anic revelation are accepted as they stand. In particular the Qur'an will not be treated as the product of Muhammad's consciousness. As we proceed, however, it will be necessary to distinguish between the actual assertions of the Qur'an and the deductions and inferences of later Muslim scholars and theologians.

3. The Organic Understanding of the Situation

It has been asserted above that written scriptures are not seen as an isolated phenomenon, still less the activity of revelation to which they are related, but that these scriptures and this activity are to be understood as part of a whole which also includes the response of a community. In particular Christianity is to be seen as an organic growth, developing from the Israelite religion of the Old Testament, or indeed from the pre-

8

Israelite religion of Abraham. Growth means not only matur-
ing but also expanding, both in number of adherents and in
other ways. So Christianity has grown until we now have the
vast 'body' of Christians in the world today. This process of
growth is like the growth of an organism, and so L. S. Thornton
coined the phrase 'the organism of historical Christianity'.[5]
It will be useful to elaborate this conception by distinguishing
within the organism of a historical religion between the
nucleus, the body proper and the outer body.

The nucleus or source of energy in the organism cannot be
isolated for inspection and study any more than the life of an
animal organism can be isolated. Yet it seems necessary to
postulate a nucleus of this kind to simplify our thinking. The
organism of a religion grows and expands, and the categories
of our thinking demand that it should do so through a power
or energy, and that this power should have a seat. The nucleus
is this postulated seat of power and energy. From it proceed
the activities of the organism, and it directs these activities
outwards, or rather, towards expansion and greater maturity.
The organism of a religion expands both by bringing a larger
number of people within the religious community, by bringing
further aspects of the life of the community under the control
of the religion, and by extending the influence of the religion
into the environment beyond the actual community. Greater
maturity is to be linked with a higher degree of integration
within the organism, and in this respect the nucleus acts as the
centre of unity or integration.

The body proper or inner body might perhaps be called the
endosoma. It consists of what is definitely marked off as being
'within the body' (e.g. 'within the Church'). This is to be
distinguished from the outer body, which correspondingly may
be called the ectosoma, and consists of that part of the environment which is arranged and controlled by the organism. In the
case of the organism of a human family, the endosoma would
be the persons who are members of the family, while the
ectosoma would be the house and garden ordered by the
family as the necessary base for many of its activities. Domestic
help and other persons regularly performing services for the
family might also be said to belong to the ectosoma. In the case
of the organism of a religion the ectosoma will include those

9

persons who have been influenced by the teaching of the religion and who may be thinking of joining the community, but who are definitely not within it. Much of the early expansion of Christianity was among groups of 'God-fearers' attached to Jewish synagogues in the cities of the Roman Empire – the ectosoma of Judaism, which soon became part of the endosoma of Christianity. The ectosoma may also be said to include those spheres of life extending beyond the members of the religious community over which the religion has some influence. Long before the Roman Empire became officially Christian it had become the ectosoma of the Christian organism.

This terminology will perhaps help us to bring the pursuit of scientific knowledge into relation with the religious community. This pursuit is part of the proper activity of the Christian endosoma. According to the teaching given in the first chapter of the book of *Genesis* man was created by God to 'have dominion' over all the living things in the world and also generally over all the earth. From the living things, animals and plants, he was to derive his food. In this conception, then, the relation of man to nature is brought under his religious outlook; and consequently the pursuit of scientific knowledge becomes part of the exercise of man's dominion over nature, and a proper 'religious' activity. It is not accidental that many of the early members of the Royal Society in London were clergymen.

Contemporary scientific research can still be regarded in this way by a religiously-minded scientist, but in practice a change has come over the relationship of those engaged in scientific research in regard to the Christian nucleus. The eighteenth century might be taken as the period when this change began (though there are also arguments for other dates). That section of the Christian organism which was pursuing scientific knowledge began to be estranged from the traditional intellectual leadership, for reasons which need not be discussed here, and that estrangement has continued and increased. As a consequence, scientific research has moved from the Christian endosoma to the ectosoma. The energy devoted to extending man's control over nature no longer comes directly from the Christian nucleus, though some may come in a residual way from Christianity. On the other hand, some certainly comes from the rival Marxist nucleus.

To turn back now to the Islamic religion – it is possible to speak in a similar way of 'the organism of historical Islam'. In its origins, however, the organism of Islam was not independent, but began in the ectosoma of the Christian organism, since Christian ideas were penetrating Arabia. In this ectosoma, with the preaching of Muhammad at Mecca and Medina a new nucleus appeared. Gradually it extended its control over a huge area, geographically and intellectually. Much of this area had been in the ectosoma of Christianity, some of it in the endosoma. It now became the endosoma of Islam, however, since, for reasons which are not relevant here, the Christian and Islamic organisms came to occupy completely separate regions of the world, and had very little relation with one another.

The modern situation, as already noticed, is that the world has been physically unified by means of science-based technology which was mostly developed in the Christian ectosoma. To some extent the whole world has become part of the Christian ectosoma, but the influence of the Christian nucleus on this ectosoma is probably decreasing, despite attempts at expansion through the missionary movement. At the same time there has been a resurgence of most of the great world religions, and new religions have also appeared. The Islamic nucleus is reaching out and increasing the number of adherents in its geographical ectosoma. It is even engaging in missionary work in Europe.

One might describe the present situation in a slightly different way. As a result of modern technology there has been a cultural and intellectual unification of the whole world at certain levels. The nuclei of all religions are thus challenged to extend their control over this intellectual sphere common to all the world, and so to make it part of their ectosoma. What exactly this means in practice will be considered towards the end of the book.

TWO

MUHAMMAD'S EXPERIENCE OF REVELATION

☾

1. The Experience as described in the Qur'an and the Tradition

A modern approach to the subject of this study naturally begins with the immediate human experience of Muhammad. This phrase is intended to indicate the factual element in Muhammad's experience apart from interpretation. This factual element, of course, is an ideal to which we can only approach asymptotically without ever reaching it. In all actual experience there is inevitably an element of interpretation. To some extent this can be detected and, if not entirely removed, at least replaced by other forms of interpretation more congenial to the contemporary outlook. The programme of the present study, then, is to examine the data in the Qur'an and the Traditions about Muhammad's experiences, and then try to distinguish the element of interpretation.

Near the beginning of his experiences Muhammad apparently had two visions, for these are described in the Qur'an to refute opponents' criticisms of his claims to prophethood. The passage [53.2-18] runs as follows:

Your companion did not go astray nor err;
he does not express mere fancies;
it (the message) is indeed a revelation revealed.
There taught him one of mighty power,
sound and steadfast; he stood straight
there on the highest horizon.
Then he came near and moved down –
two bow-lengths off or nearer –
and revealed to his slave what he revealed.

The heart did not fail to know what it saw;
do you (all) dispute with him about what he was seeing?
   He saw him also at a second descent
at the lote-tree of the limit,
where is the Garden of the Abode,
when there covered the lote-tree what covered it.
The eye wavered not nor exceeded.
He indeed had sight of the greatest signs of his Lord.

It is at once obvious that these are not scientific descriptions. In that of the second vision there is much that remains mysterious after all the labours of Muslim and non-Muslim scholars. Its interest in the present study is largely of a negative kind. There is no mention of any revelation to Muhammad in the course of this vision; but because, at a time when he had received many revelations, it is singled out for mention, it may be inferred that his receiving of revelations was not normally accompanied by any vision.

With regard to the first vision – briefly described also in 81.24, again as part of a defence of the truth of the revelations – the significance of the word 'slave' ('abd) must be noticed. Even Muslim commentators who hold that all revelations were brought to Muhammad by the angel Gabriel agree that it would not be proper that Muhammad should be referred to as the 'slave' of an angel, since the word 'slave' or 'servant' had also the connotation of 'worshipper'. The only being whose slave he could be was God. From this it follows that these words must originally have conveyed to the Meccan hearers the idea that in the vision Muhammad had seen God himself; and from this it would further follow that this was the belief of Muhammad and the Muslims. Such an interpretation of the vision would be very natural; and it is also likely that in course of time, through contact with Jews and Christians and in other ways, the Muslims would realize that it was widely believed that God could not be seen by man in this world – as 6.103 puts it, 'sight reaches him (God) not' – and would therefore interpret the figure seen in the angel as that of an angel.

It is also asserted that in the course of the vision there had been a revelation to Muhammad. The verb here translated 'reveal' is awḥā, which in much of the Qur'an is a technical expression for this experience of Muhammad's. There are also traces of a non-technical use. In 19.11/12 in the story of Zacharias it is stated that he went out from the sanctuary 'and *awḥā* to his people that they should glorify (God) morning and evening'. This would seem to mean making a sign with the hand or head, and might be translated 'signalled'. In pre-Islamic poetry the corresponding noun *waḥy* means 'writing' and is often used of inscriptions on stone. Another interesting usage is in the phrase 'the *waḥy* of the eyes is their speech'. Most commentators and translators treat most of the instances of the words in the Qur'an as technical, and the usual translations are 'reveal' and 'revelation'. Richard Bell, however, thinks that the word was never completely technical in the Qur'an, and prefers the translation 'suggest' and 'suggestion'. It would seem, then, that basically *waḥy* means 'communication' in a very general sense, and is not necessarily anything so precise as speech.

The difficulties of interpretation of this Qur'anic term are well illustrated by a passage in another sura [42.51/0-52]:

It befitted not a man that God should address him except by *waḥy* or from behind a veil, or should send a messenger who would 'reveal' (*awḥā*) what he will. . . . Thus we revealed (*awḥā*) to you (Muhammad) a spirit from our affair.

This indicates that there were several different 'manners' of revelation – a point taken up by later Muslim scholars. The words 'from behind a veil' presumably mean that, where this was the appropriate description, there was no accompanying vision. On the other hand, where the revelation came through a messenger, one might suppose that there was a vision of the messenger, presumably an angel; yet the absence of any descriptions of angelic visions makes the supposition dubious, and it may be that Muhammad was aware of the angel in some indirect way. It appears impossible to be more precise than this about the meaning of the Qur'anic phrases.

A different aspect of the revelation is indicated by the verbal forms *nazzala* and *anzala*, both meaning 'to send down', and together occurring three times as often in the Qur'an as *awḥā* and its derivatives. The idea of 'sending down' implies that there are messengers who bear the messages or revelations from God to the prophets. Sometimes the messengers are spoken of as angels simply, as in the following verses: 'we (God) do not send down the angels except with the truth' [15.8]; 'we (sc. the angels) do not come down except by the command of your Lord' [19.64/5]. Sometimes a mysterious being called 'the spirit' is associated with the angels: 'there come down the angels and the spirit in (that night) by the permission of their Lord . . .' [97.4]. Yet again the spirit is mentioned alone: 'the spirit of holiness causes it to come down from your Lord with truth' [16.102/4]. Finally, Jibrīl or Gabriel is named as the messenger (and presumably identified with 'the spirit'): 'Gabriel caused it to come down on your heart by God's permission' [2.97/1].

The chief conclusion from all this discussion is that the prophetic experience was not all of a type, but varied from time to time. Latterly, however, it may have come to approximate to a single norm, which is the 'manner' expressed in the last quotation. The essential features in this experience appear to be: (1) Muhammad is aware that certain words are present in his 'heart' or conscious mind; (2) they are not the result of any conscious thinking processes on his part; (3) he believes them to be placed in his mind by an external agency which he speaks of as an angel; (4) he believes that the message is ultimately from God. These four features would seem to be present in all the 'manners' of revelation described in the Qur'an, with two provisos: firstly, in regard to (1), there may have been some cases in which the words came to be present in his mind because he had heard them; and secondly, in regard to (3), the external agency need not always have been conceived as an angel. Perhaps the absolutely essential features might be reduced to three: the words in his conscious mind; the absence of his own thinking; and the belief that the words were from God.

The same features are found, along with various picturesque details, in the Traditions. This material need only be mentioned briefly, since it adds nothing essential to the Qur'an, and since its additions are looked on with suspicion by most modern scholars. Thus there is a Tradition, occurring in several forms, about Muhammad's call to be a prophet. The main part of this story is that an angel appeared to Muhammad and said, 'I am Gabriel, and you are the Messenger of God.' Then he went on,

'Recite'. Muhammad said, 'What shall I recite?' The angel replied, 'Recite in the name of your Lord, who created. . . .' This is the beginning of sura 96, which is usually held to have been the first sura revealed. The story might conceivably be one account (with interpretative additions, like the mention of Gabriel) of the experience connected with the first of the visions described in sura 53.[1]

Another Tradition represents Muhammad, in reply to a question, describing various 'manners' of his experience of revelation. 'Sometimes it comes to me like the reverberation of a bell,' he said, 'and that is hardest on me; then it (the unusual state) passes from me, and I have present in mind from it what he (God?) said; and sometimes the angel takes the form of a man for me, and addresses me, and I have present in mind what he says.' His favourite wife 'Ā'isha told how, even on a very cold day, she had seen his forehead streaming with perspiration at the coming of the revelation.[2] These stories have the same basic features of the experience of revelation. The physical and psychological accompaniments are interesting, and may well be authentic; but they need not be further discussed here, since, even if they are authentic, they do not prove that Muhammad really received messages from God; similarly, if they are not authentic, their absence does not prove that he did not receive such messages.

Of the three features of the experience of revelation mentioned above, the first two are already formulated in neutral terms, that is, with a minimum of interpretation. Muhammad found words or verbal contents in his consciousness; these he remembered, and they were eventually written down and constitute the Qur'an as we have it. Secondly, Muhammad was aware of no conscious thinking from which these verbal contents might result; in other words, he believed he could distinguish them from his conscious thinking. So far the description of the experience is at the psychological level. The remaining feature, however, the belief that the verbal contents came from God, is interpretative and not something sensuously experienced, probably not even imaginatively experienced. It is in part an inference from the absence of Muhammad's own conscious thinking, and also from the nature of the verbal contents.

A fashionable modern way of formulating the first feature

would be to say that the verbal contents came into Muhammad's consciousness from the unconscious. Such a formulation might be relatively neutral, but then it would only mean that it was not known where the verbal contents came from. On the other hand, if it presupposed a Freudian or Jungian theory of the unconscious, there would be an interpretative element. The whole discussion of interpretations, theistic and psychological, of Muhammad's experience will be deferred to the second half of Chapter 9. Meanwhile we proceed on the basis of an acceptance of the first two features. That is to say, we shall hold that the verbal contents now constituting the Qur'an appeared mysteriously from time to time in Muhammad's conscious mind, and were *not* in any way the product of his own thinking. This will mean that it will be incorrect to say of a Qur'anic verse that 'Muhammad said such and such a thing'. On the other hand, it may fairly be presumed with all Muslim scholars that, once the Qur'anic verses had mysteriously appeared in Muhammad's mind, he accepted them as true. In this way the Qur'an gives us insight into what Muhammad thought. Moreover, as emphasized frequently in this study, because the Qur'an is addressed to Muhammad or the Muslims or their pagan contemporaries, it presupposes the particular mentality of each group, and in this way gives us insight into what each was thinking.

2. The Possibility of Revision

On the basis of the attitude towards Muhammad's experience of revelation just described, there can of course be no question of Muhammad consciously revising the Qur'an.[3] Some European scholars in the past have spoken as if Muhammad did this, and this way of speaking is to be regretted. It is also unscholarly in that it fails to take into account the essential phenomenological features of Muhammad's experience. In the present 'interreligious' atmosphere it is particularly important that non-Muslims should avoid both speaking and thinking in this way. When all this has been said, however, there are still several ways open in which a revision of the Qur'an might have taken place. The simplest way would be by a new revelation supplementing the previous one. For instance, it is conceivable that some of the verses containing criticisms of Jews and Christians spoke only of the Jews when they were originally revealed, since in the early years at Medina there was much opposition from Jews and practically none from Christians. At a later period when there was Christian opposition the verse may have been revealed again, but with the addition of the words 'and Christians'; and Muhammad or those who later 'collected' the Qur'an may have included only the later and fuller form. Admittedly there is no way of proving that this is what happened. It is only a hypothesis; but it is part of the modern scientific outlook to proceed on the basis of such hypotheses. In the hypothesis itself, however, there is nothing contrary to the essential beliefs of Muslims.

Although the particular form of revision just suggested is hypothetical, the Qur'an itself speaks of processes which are tantamount to revision. In particular there are verses which form the basis of the theory of 'abrogation' worked out by Muslim scholars. In Arabic this is usually known as *an-nāsikh wa-l-mansūkh*, 'the abrogating and the abrogated'. The theory is that some of the commands given by God in the Qur'an to Muhammad and the Muslims were only applicable for a limited period. Thus the earlier part of sura 73, commanding the Muslims to spend a large part of the night in prayer was only applicable while they were at Mecca; accordingly at Medina the last verse of the sura was revealed, and this abrogates the command in the first part of the sura. The verses abrogated in this way, however, are retained in the Qur'an.

The verb used for 'abrogate', *nasakha*, occurs twice with this sense in the Qur'an, though it seems more appropriate there to give the more general sense of 'cancel'.

Wherever we (God) cancel a verse or cause its forgetting, we bring a better than it or the like of it [2.106/0].

Before you (Muhammad) we sent no messenger nor prophet, but that, when he recited (verses), Satan threw something into his recitation; so God cancelled what Satan threw in; then God adjusts his verses . . . that he may make what Satan threw in a test for the diseased of heart and the hard-hearted . . . and that those given knowledge may know it is the truth from your Lord and may believe in it [22.52/1].

18

The words here translated 'recite' and 'recitation' are not the usual ones; they appear to refer to some particular aspect of Muhammad's experience of revelation, but the precise interpretation does not affect the present point.

The second of these passages is usually illustrated by the story of the 'satanic verses'.[4] The story is that, while Muhammad was wondering how his religion might be made easier for the Meccans to accept, he began to receive the revelation with the words [53.19, 20]: 'Have you considered al-Lāt and al-'Uzzā, and Manāt, the third, the other?' Then at this point Satan threw on to his tongue the words 'These are the cranes exalted, whose intercession is to be hoped for'. This was taken by the pagan Meccans as permitting the worship of their deities to the extent of praying them to intercede with the supreme God on behalf of the worshippers. Thereupon they all joined Muhammad in his worship. Later, however, it became clear that such intercession was not in accordance with Islamic monotheism, and Muhammad received the true continuation of these two verses – what is now found in the Qur'an. It is implicit in this story (whose general truth is vouched for by the Qur'anic passage quoted) that the 'satanic verses' were never part of the Qur'an; and not surprisingly they are absent from the present text. For this reason 'cancel' in 22.52/1 must mean more than 'abrogate'. In 2.106/0, on the other hand, where 'cancel' is distinguished from 'cause to forget' (which would lead to disappearance from the Qur'an), the word 'cancel' might well have the sense of 'abrogate'.

Apart from these instances of the technical word for 'abrogate', there are other passages where comparable ideas are expressed:

God effaces what he will or establishes (it); and with
him is the 'mother' of the book [13.37].
When we put a verse in place of another – and God
knows best what he sends down – they say, You
(Muhammad) are only an inventor . . . [16.101/3].
If we will, we shall indeed take away what we have
revealed to you [17.86/8].

The Qur'an also envisages the possibility that Muhammad may forget some of the passages revealed to him; and this does not imply any failure or weakness on his part, but, as 2.106/0 suggests, may have been brought about by God. Other two references to Muhammad's forgetting might be understood in the same way:

> We shall cause you to recite, and you shall not forget except what God wills . . . [87.6 f.].
> . . . and remember your Lord when you forget, and say, Perhaps my Lord will lead me to something nearer true guidance than this [18.24/3].

In all these ways, then, the Qur'an contemplates what is tantamount to revision. This may come about by the cancellation or abrogation of verses, and also by God's causing them to be forgotten and replacing them by others. What was described in the first paragraph of this section as a hypothesis – one revelation revising another – could be described in Qur'anic terms as the cancellation or forgetting of the original revelation and its replacement by the 'revised' revelation.

Perhaps the most important point is the implication that the revelations are adapted to the changing needs of the community. The initial positive responses to the first revelations by Muhammad and the first Muslims led to the founding of a community. As this community grew and met opposition, it required further guidance; and this came in the fresh revelations received by Muhammad from time to time. Whatever name is given to these processes that have been described here, they are certainly the adaptation of the revealed message to the life of a growing community.

3. The 'Collection' of the Qur'an

There is a well-known tradition about the first 'collection' of the Qur'an. According to the most usual form of this tradition 'Umar ibn-al-Khaṭṭāb (who later was caliph from 634 to 644) noticed that many 'reciters' of the Qur'an had been killed in the battle of the Yamama (about 633), and became anxious lest some of the Qur'an should be lost for ever. He therefore approached the caliph Abū-Bakr and suggested that he should arrange for the 'collection' of the Qur'an. Abū-Bakr thereupon commissioned Zayd ibn-Thābit to do this. Zayd proceeded to gather portions of the Qur'an from 'pieces of papyrus, flat stones, palm-branches, shoulder-blades and ribs of animals, bits of leather, wooden tablets and the hearts of men.' When he had written everything out on leaves of the same size, he gave these to Abū-Bakr, on whose death they went to 'Umar, who entrusted them to his daughter Ḥafṣa.

This 'collection' does not appear to have been very effective, for about 650 (in the caliphate of 'Uthmān), following on disputes in the army about the text to be used in worship, 'Uthmān commissioned Zayd and three Meccans to make another 'collection' of the Qur'an, using the leaves in the possession of Ḥafṣa. The new 'collection' was duly completed, and certified copies of it sent to the main centres of the Islamic Empire, with the instruction that all other texts were to be destroyed. It is this official 'Uthmanic version which is in our hands today. Despite the order to destroy other versions, however, many traces have remained of these pre-'Uthmanic codices (maṣāḥif). The best-known and most important was that of Ibn-Masʿūd. Variant readings from these codices are mentioned in the Muslim commentaries on the Qur'an. Muslim scholars studied the readings in the old codices, and one book on this topic – Kitāb al-maṣāḥif by Abū-Bakr 'Abd-Allāh ibn-Abī-Dā'ūd Sulaymān ibn-al-Ashʿath as-Sijistānī (d. 928/316) – has been edited and studied by Arthur Jeffery in his Materials for the History of the Text of the Qur'ān (Leiden, 1937).

It is clear that the final result of all this process described as 'collection' was the production of the text of the Qur'an which we now have, but it is not clear what exactly the process was. The word 'collect' is probably used because it occurs in an important passage [75.16-19]:

Move not your tongue in it to hasten with it;
ours is the collecting of it and the reciting of it.
When we recite it, follow the reciting of it.
Then ours is the explaining of it.

There is much that is mysterious in this passage, and Muslim commentators have had some difficulty in finding an interpretation that is in accordance with the usual view or assumption that before Zayd there was nothing done towards the 'collecting' of the Qur'an. The natural interpretation of the passage, however, would be that, just as Muhammad followed the divine initiative in the reciting of the Qur'an, so also he followed it in the *jam'* or 'collecting', that is, the joining together of pieces that had already been revealed separately. Unless Muhammad had thus occupied himself in 'collecting' the Qur'an, it is difficult to see how Zayd or any other Muslim would have had the presumption to undertake something which the Qur'an asserted was reserved to God. If, on the other hand, Muhammad following divine inspiration had accomplished the greater part of the work, it would not be unduly presumptuous to complete the work in accordance with the principle on which he had operated.

It seems likely, then, that many of the suras received most of the form they now have from Muhammad himself. It is held that only one sura was sent down as a single revelation; but the Qur'anic challenges to opponents to produce suras[5] imply that the Muslims already possessed some suras (presumably in their memories), and further that Muhammad produced these by joining together separate revelations. Such a view, which seems to be required by the Qur'an itself, in no way eliminates the work of Zayd. Even if the bulk – say four fifths – of the Qur'an had been given its present form by Muhammad, Zayd may well have found a large number of small passages of two or three verses on a variety of writing materials; and it would be far from easy to know where all these passages should go. It also seems very likely that in 'the hearts of men' Zayd found passages which began in the same way but had different endings. The existence of such alternative endings is a feature of which the modern reader soon becomes aware. Presumably there were in fact revelations which began in the same way but ended differently. The problem for the 'collector' would be whether to repeat the whole each time, or to be content with what was different. It would seem that sometimes the one procedure and sometimes the other was adopted. Another part of the work of the 'collectors' would be to put the suras in a definite order; reports about the codex of Ibn-Mas'ūd show that the order there was rather different.

It is not necessary to discuss in detail here the credibility of the stories of the two 'collections'. Modern European scholars have doubted much of the account of the first 'collection' under Abū-Bakr, especially because the fact that the leaves were eventually given to Ḥafṣa seems to indicate that it was not in any way official. It may well be the case, however, that at this period Zayd brought together as much material as he could find, but 'unofficially'. This doubtless left much work to be done before the final 'Uthmanic text was ready. One of the tasks of Zayd's Meccan associates was to see that deviant forms were assimilated to the dialect of Quraysh. What must rather be emphasized here is that the awareness of the need for a definitive text of the Qur'an is itself a recognition of the important place the Qur'an has in the life of the community. Men who controlled the policies of a rapidly expanding empire had no time for purely academic accuracy. They insisted on having one definite text of the Qur'an because they realized that the community of Muslims was based on its continuing response to the divine initiative which was the revealing of the Qur'an.

The 'Uthmanic recension of the Qur'an, though it did not immediately eliminate the variants in the old codices, eventually came to be universally accepted by Muslims. In the course of time, however, there came to be many variations in the reading of the 'Uthmanic text. This came about because of the nature of Arabic writing at that period. Only consonants were written, and the dots distinguishing consonants with a similar outline were often omitted; and this made it possible to read the same consonantal outline in several different ways, all of which made sense. Another defect was that the ends of verses were not marked. Gradually improvements were made in the actual writing of the Qur'an, but before this happened several different systems of reading the consonantal outline had become widely accepted. The merit of having brought order into this confusion is ascribed to Ibn-Mujāhid (d. 935). The systems of reading of seven men, each according to two transmitters, were accepted as canonical. Three further systems were also recognized, which might be called deutero-canonical; and with the Seven these made the Ten. A slight degree of recognition was also given to 'the Four after the Ten'. Although the Seven are all equally canonical, one – that of 'Āṣim as transmitted by Ḥafṣ – has become very widely adopted by Muslims to the exclusion of most of the others.

Finally, it must be emphasized that, though there is a wealth of variant readings, none of them affect the general teaching of the Qur'an to any appreciable extent. This is the case also with the variants in the pre-'Uthmanic codices, as may be seen by looking at the lists in the book by Arthur Jeffery mentioned above. In a way the recognition of the canonicity of the seven different systems is an admission that slight textual variations (to the extent allowed) do not affect the general life of the community in its response to revelation. A contemporary of Ibn-Mujāhid claimed that it was permissible to read the consonantal outline in any way that was linguistically possible; but this view was condemned, and only reading according to one of the recognized systems officially accepted. In so far as the variants had arisen in the course of the community's response to the divine initiative they were in accordance with this response, and could not alter its general character.

THREE

THE PRESUPPOSITIONS OF THE QUR'ANIC REVELATION

❧

1. The Implications of 'an Arabic Qur'an'

In the Qur'an itself the phrase 'an Arabic Qur'an' is used five times of the revelation to Muhammad; and this phrase has implications which have not yet been fully realized by Muslims, but which are of the greatest importance in the contemporary 'interreligious' world. The fundamental point is that the Qur'an is addressed (through Muhammad) to people who understand Arabic, and therefore must be intelligible to them. This means much more than the use of words familiar to the Arabs of the early sixth century. The whole life of a people is implicit in its use of language, especially the cultural and intellectual milieu, with its distinctive categories of thinking, its specific world-view, its aesthetic and ethical values, its historical conceptions. It was for long the view of most Muslim scholars that the Qur'an is untranslatable. When one thinks of the many unique aspects of the life of the Arabs, one may agree with this view. A genuine understanding of the Qur'an requires familiarity with the distinctive features of Arab life, especially in the desert, and with Arab ways of thinking.

Every language enshrines the past experience of the cultural milieu in which it has developed. In particular the Arabic language is closely connected with the life of the Arabs in the desert including all its unpredictability, all the hardships that have to be patiently endured, and the overriding need for solidarity in the kin-group. Yet Arabic is not restricted to the life of the desert. Legend (with some basis in fact) tells of an earlier agricultural life before men took to the desert, of the breakdown of the irrigation system in the Yemen and of the departure of various tribes from that once pleasant land. These

experiences must be presumed to have left traces in the con-
notations of various words. Then there were many Arabs
engaged in trading and commerce; the great merchants of
Mecca controlled camel caravans which went regularly to Syria
in the north and the Yemen in the south, the latter to link with
the trade routes to the Indies and East Africa. Such commerce
also left its mark on the Arabic language.

Thus the Arabic language is linked with a special cultural
milieu, which has many features which distinguish it from
other cultural milieus. This is a fact of great importance, especially in the 'interreligious' world. It means that there is no
'standard' man, but various 'standard' men, each from a distinctive cultural region. Even in the Islamic world there are
local variations within a single cultural pattern, so that hostile
critics say that there is no such thing as Islam, but that there is
a different Islam in each country. Sometimes these differences
may express themselves in religious sectarianism, sometimes
in other ways. Even the spoken Arabic language varies from
country to country, while the outlook of the middle-class
citizen of Cairo differs enormously from that of the average
inhabitant of a town in the centre of Arabia like Riyadh or
Hail. For the purposes of this study, however, these differences
within the Arabic cultural milieu may be neglected. Our
primary concern is with what is common to all Arabs, or at
least to all Arabic-speaking Muslims.

The Qur'an asserts that the message brought by Muhammad
to his people was the same as that brought by other prophets
to their peoples. It would seem, however, that this can only
refer to the essentials of the message, such as belief in God and
in the Last Day, and in prophets, angels and books. Some
Muslim scholars might argue that the differences between the
Qur'an and the Old and New Testaments are due to the
'corruption' of these books by Jews and Christians; but it
would seem that what the Qur'an itself says about the 'corruption' of previous scriptures is much less than what is asserted
in the theories of later Muslims.[1] Quite apart from this theory,
however, the Qur'an itself makes it clear that it is not a repetition
in Arabic of the detailed contents of other revealed books.
Much of it is addressed specifically to Arabs – as sura 106 is
addressed specifically to the tribe of Quraysh. Much of it, too,

shows the Muslims the proper attitude to adopt to various events in the life of the community — the great success at Badr, the reverse at Uhud, the disappointing behaviour of the nomads, and so on. These are references to contemporary events and situations, and cannot be repetitions of any previous scripture.

The basic problem here is that of the relation of divine universality to human particularity; and this might also be approached in another way. It might be held, for instance, that the particular events of Muhammad's lifetime were spoken of in the Qur'an because they exemplified and typified fundamental aspects of human experience. It would follow that the assertions of the Qur'an, while having a particular reference, yet have a universal character; and for this reason, it would be further argued, the Qur'an is addressed to man universally, and not simply to man in the Arab cultural milieu. This is a powerful argument, for the Islamic religion has expanded far beyond the original confines of the Arab cultural milieu, and has gained devoted adherents from many races and environments. There is a short reply, however, to the claim that Islam is for man universally, namely, that there are many cultural regions which it has not yet penetrated or not to any significant degree. These are the cultural regions where the other great world-religions are dominant. It is not impossible, of course, that some day the majority of the inhabitants of these regions will be converted to Islam; but it is also possible that Islam will fail to make any appreciable headway there. All that one is justified in concluding, then, is that in the past Islam has expanded far beyond the Arab milieu in the strict sense, and that there is nothing to show that further expansion is impossible.

There are two points, however, which ought to be considered here with respect to Islamic expansion in the past. One is the possibility that the non-Arab regions into which Islam expanded were culturally similar to the Arab milieu, and that this facilitated the expansion. The other is the undoubted fact that in the regions where Islam is the dominant religion, the local culture has been greatly influenced by Arab culture, and sometimes largely replaced by it. With regard to the first point, it is obvious that certain cultural dissimilarities will hinder the spread of Islam. Thus there are certain East African tribes where circumcision was thought to make a man unfit for marriage; and, while this belief continued to be held, it was difficult for the men to become Muslims. At a deeper level it would seem that where men (the Greeks, for example) held a dualistic conception of man as consisting of soul and body, they would find it hard to accept Qur'anic teaching, which is based on a monistic conception of man whereby the body is as much the man as the soul. For a time, it is true, some Muslims accepted Greek philosophy, where the dualistic conception of man tends to prevail; but in the end Greek theories were rejected by the great mass of Muslims. It would appear then that certain cultural regions were more hospitable to Islam than others; but this first point is not altogether independent of the second.

The expansion of what may be called the Qur'anic mentality into the regions where Islam has become the dominant religion is a phenomenon worthy of further detailed study, as are the comparable developments in other cultural regions. The military expansion of the Arabs led to the spread of the Arab race, especially when only descent in the male line was taken into account. The Arabic language also spread, and was adopted even by those who had no claim to Arab descent, and by non-Muslims such as the Copts of Egypt. Those Muslim populations which retained their own languages inevitably incorporated many Arabic words into them. This is the case with Persian, Turkish, Urdu, Malay, Swahili and Hausa. These Muslims who have retained their former language must, along with the language, have retained something of their former mentality. Until much further study is done, it is impossible to say much about this in detail; but one has the impression that throughout the Islamic world there is something of a common Islamic mentality.

The conclusion of these reflections is that at the present time there is a distinctive Islamic cultural region, clearly marked off from the other cultural regions in the world. The mentality of this region has been largely formed by the Arabic milieu in which the Qur'an first appeared. To the people of this cultural region the Islamic religion appears more satisfactory than any other. It is indeed the religion appropriate to their mentality; and this is not surprising, since the religion has helped to form the mentality. What is important in the present study is the relationship of the Qur'an to this Islamic mentality, and more especially to the Arab mentality out of which the Islamic mentality has grown. The special relation of the Qur'an to the Arab mentality is implied by the phrase 'an Arabic Qur'an'.

By holding firmly to this fact that the Qur'an is addressed in the first place to Arabs of the early seventh century, it is possible to give an account of the 'sources' of Qur'anic thought that should be less objectionable to Muslims than much of what has been said by European scholars in the past. Nineteenth-century scholarship may be said to have been obsessed by the search for sources. The idea of development was in the air, and by a certain confusion of thought it was supposed that, if you had shown what a thing originally was, or what it was derived from, you had provided the most important clues to an understanding of what it really was. The fallacy of this view is shown if we look at Shakespeare's 'sources' for *Hamlet* – the story-material that he had presumably read. When we compare the 'sources' with the finished product, we have further insight into the working of Shakespeare's genius; but virtually nothing is added to our appreciation of the play itself.

Something similar is true of the Qur'an, provided that we keep in mind that it is not to be regarded as a work of human genius. This means that we cannot speak of the 'sources' of the Qur'an itself. On the other hand, since the Qur'an is addressed to Arabs who were Muhammad's contemporaries, it is legitimate to ask – even from a strictly Muslim point of view – how far the Arab mentality of the time had been influenced by Jewish or Christian ideas, or by other forms of thought present in the Middle East of that day. Many Arabs had been in touch with the Byzantine Empire in one way or another, and had doubtless become familiar with Greek and Christian ideas. Persian influences can be traced in the language of pre-Islamic poetry. The people of Medina had learned many things from the Jews settled there. These 'sources' of the mentality of the pre-Islamic Arabs do not tell us much about it; but they contribute a little to our understanding of the cultural processes of the time. They tell us nothing about how the Qur'an was conveyed to Muhammad. It must be assumed, however, that the Qur'an was addressed to the Arabs just as they were, slightly influenced by certain Jewish and Christian ideas, and vaguely aware of the great civilizations beyond Arabia.

2. Categorial Presuppositions

The Arab mentality is distinguished from others – as these are distinguished from one another – by its categorial presuppositions. These presuppositions are not matters belonging to the content of the thinking of Arabs, but the categories or forms of thought in which this thinking is expressed. These forms of thought are so general that the ordinary man, living in a community of people with a similar mentality, is usually unaware of the part they play in his thinking. The same may even be true to some extent of the academic thinker. In the contemporary world, however, where a man meets many people from a different cultural milieu, arguments will often be at cross purposes until men realize that their basic differences are categorial ones. The following pages, therefore, should only be regarded as a preliminary essay in this field. Some of the points will be illustrated from the Qur'an, but others, such as the attitude to logical consistency, really only appear later. As is natural, many will be closely related to features of Arabic grammar.

As a first point one might take the primacy of personal relationships in Arab thinking. It is a common experience of those who have contacts with Arabs, even Arabs from the great cities of the Middle East, that they have a much keener awareness of personal relationships than the average European. This may, of course, be due to the fact that as a nation they have been immersed for a shorter period of time in the materialism of an advanced technological society. On the other hand, the concern with persons may have a deeper root than this. Perhaps it would not be fanciful to take a grammatical phenomenon as indicative of something fundamental to the Arab mentality. The simple English sentence 'he brought the thing to John' becomes in Arabic 'he came-to John with the thing' (*ātā-hu bi-sh-shay'*). It is also normal in Arabic to have verbs of coming and going with a person as direct object. If we may generalize from this, it would seem that in Arabic, where my activity affects both a person and a thing, the person is given the primacy by being made direct object of the verb, while the thing is secondary by being made an indirect object. In English, on the other hand, the thing appears to be primary and the person secondary. There is, of course, in English the possibility of saying 'he approached John with the gift'; but most of the simple verbs of motion are intransitive. In these cases, then, Arabic would appear to be more person-directed and less thing-directed than English. At bottom this must go back to the fundamental conception of human activity.

Probably connected with this difference is the Arabic analysis of the temporal aspect of activity, as seen in the system of grammatical tenses. We Europeans tend to think of time in the categories of past, present and future; and we find these categories in our grammatical forms. This might be described as a lineal or mathematical conception of time. Now it is possible to some extent to analyse Arabic grammatical forms into past, present and future; but if one begins with the forms themselves they direct one to a very different analysis, namely an analysis into 'completed action' and 'incomplete action'. The forms indicating incomplete action can be used with reference to the past, the present and the future. The forms indicating completed action can be used of the future when the action is thought of as already realized (*sc.* because it is certain that it will be realized). As contrasted with the abstract European conception of time, this analysis would appear to be based on the conception of experienced time. In human experience there is a time of planning and a time of achievement, or, more generally, a time when life is still indeterminate and a time when it has become determined. One might look for some connection with the life of the Arabs in the desert, where plans so often go wrong that much planning is futile, and the chief distinction is between the indeterminate and the determined.

Yet another aspect of human activity is the distinction between being active and being passive. Perhaps in the life of the desert there was a basic awareness of the narrow limits within which man can act effectively. We have our own belief that 'man proposes, but God disposes'; but in Arabian experience this principle was more far-reaching. It was held that man's food or sustenance (*rizq*) was predetermined, and also the term (*ajal*) of his life, that is, the date of his death; no matter how a man acted these would not be altered. This experience must have affected the whole conception of acting or being an agent. The agent by doing something contributes to the process by which the indeterminate passes into the determined, but the determined is not necessarily a realization of the agent's ends. With this point is perhaps to be connected the conception of responsibility current among many Muslims, which is essentially an external or physical responsibility. Even today, if a taxi-driver runs over a child, it is normal, though everyone admits it was entirely the child's fault, for the taxi-driver to have to pay blood-money, since the death proceeded from his physical act.

There is a curious feature about the Arabic verbal forms which take the place of the passive voice in English verbs. The form is termed the 'unknown' (*majhūl*), because the agent of the action is not known. Such a sentence as *qutila Zayd* is normally translated 'Zayd was killed'; but it might perhaps be better to translate it 'someone killed Zayd'. If one wants to mention the killer, this form cannot be used. That is, one cannot translate directly into Arabic 'Zayd was killed by Aswad', but must put it actively, 'Aswad killed Zayd'. This usage may be linked with the point about the primacy of the personal; to say 'by Aswad' might be taken as treating Aswad as if he were a kind of instrument. What all is implied in this conception? Man's agency may be thought of in an external way without reference to the agent's ends. Yet there is a pride in being human. Whatever powers overrule man's ends, they do not treat man as he treats his sword or his knife. Sometimes one may not know the person chiefly concerned in the passage of the indeterminate into the determined; but if we know him and want to mention him, we must mention him properly as an agent.

Another set of categories are those concerned with regularity and irregularity in nature and history. Unlike agricultural populations dependent on the seasons, the Arabian nomad seems to be less aware of the regularities of nature than of its irregularities. Rainfall in particular tends to be erratic in Arabia. In a given year it may be plentiful in one valley, and negligible

32

in another not far away; and then this distribution of rainfall may be reversed in the following year. Because of this the movements of the nomads may vary from year to year. In such circumstances it is not surprising that the Arabs have little idea of the regularities and laws of nature.

This absence of regularity may have something to do with the atomistic tendency which appeared in later Islamic thinking. This is the tendency to regard each event, not as part of a continuing process, but as something which exists by itself in isolation. The extreme form of atomistic view leads to the assertion, for example, that the tree before me at the present moment will not be there in the next moment of time unless God creates its existence in this further moment. This tendency to adopt atomistic conceptions may in part be due to other factors, such as the Islamic conception of God; but, whatever the source, it long played an important part in Islamic theology. The emphasis was on the discontinuity in nature, and not on smooth linear progress.

Perhaps it was because nature was thought of as discontinuous that much emphasis was placed on the need for continuity in human affairs. As is well known the greater part of the Islamic community calls itself Sunnite, because it claims to follow the *sunna* or standard practice of Muhammad. This conception, however, goes back to pre-Islamic times. The nomadic tribe was very conservative and considered that its safety and prosperity depended on its following the *sunna* of its ancestors, that is, their normal methods of dealing with the various problems of life. Now *sunna* originally means a 'beaten track'; and, if one reflects, one realizes how important it is for the traveller in the desert to stick to the beaten track. If he strays from it, he may lose his way and his life. This conception colours much later Islamic thinking. A theological heresy is called an 'innovation' (*bid'a*). The first phrase used to express the conception of 'law of nature' was 'the *sunna* of God'. Thus the Muslim comes to a new way of regarding the relation between things and persons: things are erratic and unreliable, while regularity, steadfastness and continuity are to be found above all in the human will. The regularity in nature is imposed on it by God's will, thought of as analogous to a human will.

C   33

These lines of thought come together in the Qur'anic conception of the historical process, at least in some of its aspects. For the nomadic Arab history was no more than the rise and fall of numerous tribes. There was no awareness of any continuous line of development running through it. The relative dates of the various tribes hardly mattered. History was essentially the repetition of a thematic pattern. In the Qur'an, under the influence of theism, this pattern came to be that a tribe rose to prominence and prosperity, that there came to it a messenger from God, that it disobeyed the divine message, and eventually was punished by complete destruction. This repetition of a theme has deep roots in Semitic thought, and has sometimes been given a prominent place in the interpretation of the Old Testament. It may be said to be a fundamental form of the uniformity or indeed unity of the temporal process.[2] A further study of this point in relation to Islam would seem to be well worth while, but would be out of place here.

Another categorial presupposition of the Arab mentality is related to logical consistency. In our modern scientific age it is assumed that, if a theory is inconsistent with itself, it must be wrong. Behind this lie more fundamental assumptions which have not been recognized as such. The chief of these is that human thinking is an adequate instrument to deal with the objects which man seeks to know. In some spheres, especially in those matters studied by the sciences, this assumption may be justified. There is another sphere, however – the sphere of aesthetic and ethical value and of the meaning of life – in which logical consistency is less important. We do not demand of a poet that he should be logically consistent. Such a demand is appropriate where one is dealing with abstract concepts. If a thinker puts forward a cosmology in abstract terms, we rightly require consistency. Our abstract conceptions, however, always fall short of the richness and complexity of the real world, because the human intellect for all its great power is subject to many limitations. Much of this was realized by the later Ḥanbalite theologians in Islam when they avoided the abstract conceptions of the Ash'arites and others and clung to the concrete terms of the Qur'an and the Traditions. It would follow from this that, if we discover some inconsistency in the

34

Qur'an, it is a sign of its richness and of its fruitful transcendence of barren conceptual thought. Two inconsistent statements may be retained because neither by itself fully expresses the reality; rather each brings out an aspect omitted by the other. Thus the two statements, though not logically reconcilable, together give a fuller picture of reality. Something would be lost by omitting one of them.

A final point is the Arab attitude to names and, more generally, to verbal contents. There have been parallels to this, of course, among other peoples. Among other things it was felt that the relation of a name to a thing was not accidental or conventional, but that there was a special fitness in the application of a particular name to a particular object. There is probably some truth in this view, though it may be lost in the misty origins of language. It appears in the Qur'an in the story of how Adam gave names to things [2.30/28-33/1]. In the book of *Genesis* also there is a story of how he gave names to things [2.19, 20]; but in this story it is Adam who says what the names are, and the story is at least compatible with the view that names are merely conventional. In the Qur'an, on the contrary, Adam himself has to be taught the names by God before he can tell them to the angels. It seems to be presupposed here that knowledge of the name includes a knowledge of the real nature of a thing and that there is a closer link than mere convention between the name and the nature of the thing. This was presumably a presupposition belonging to the mentality of the pre-Islamic Arabs.

It was doubtless some aspect of the same conception which led later Muslim scholars to insist on adherence to the precise verbal form in Traditions; they held it unsatisfactory to give the sense of an anecdote in other words. From the standpoint of the religion of Islam there was indeed always something God-given about language. When the critics of Muhammad are challenged to produce a sura like the ones revealed to him, the assumption is that, because these are from God, they cannot be equalled by man. It is doubtless not by chance, too, that the same word *āya* is used for 'sign' (of divine power) and 'verse' (of the revelation).

This list of categorial presuppositions underlying the Qur'an is not based on an exhaustive study of the subject, and is thus no more than a preliminary survey. It is sufficient, however, to illustrate what is meant when one speaks about a distinctive mentality among the pre-Islamic and early Islamic Arabs. This list gives strong support to the standard view of Muslim doctors that it is impossible to translate the Qur'an from Arabic into another language, and so improper to attempt it (though nowadays 'interpretations' or 'explanations' in another language are permissible and indeed desirable). The conclusion here, of course, is not restricted to the Arab mentality. Presumably we must also hold that every great cultural region has its own distinctive categorial presuppositions.

3. Cosmological Presuppositions

The categorial presuppositions are by no means the only distinctive features of the mentality of the pre-Islamic Arabs. These men also had a world-view or cosmology. We need not suppose that this was a single coherent system. General considerations and a study of the Qur'an alike suggest that there was current in Arabia an amalgam of ideas from various sources. The basis was doubtless the world-view of earlier generations of Semites, which was also the basis of the cosmological presuppositions of the Old Testament. To this had been added later Jewish, Christian-Greek and Persian-Zoroastrian ideas. These ideas were all present in various degrees in the minds of Muhammad's contemporaries, the men to whom the Qur'an was first addressed.

Most of the Arabs of Muhammad's time, both town-dwellers and nomads, must be classified as pagans, though (as has been indicated elsewhere) their effective religion was a tribal paganism. In cosmology they believed that many aspects of a man's life – such as his sustenance, the date of his death, and whether his life as a whole was happy or unhappy – were determined or predetermined by an ineluctable power which they usually referred to as 'time' (*zamān, dahr*) or 'the days'. This was not a divinity to be worshipped, but a cosmological power to be reckoned with. In a verse of the Qur'an [45.24/3] the pagans are represented as saying: 'There is only our present life; we die and we live; and Time (*dahr*) alone destroys us'. The cosmological idea that man's sustenance, death-date and degree of happiness are fixed and determined (and that nothing he can do will alter them) was taken over by Islam, but these matters were said to be determined by God and not by Time. There is even a Tradition (not well attested) in which God is represented as saying 'I am *dahr*'. There was some hesitation on man's inability to alter his final destiny. Many held that man's eventual assignment to heaven or hell depended on whether he obeyed God or not, and, though they severely limited man's freedom, many also held that man was in some sense responsible for his acts. Thus not merely does the Qur'an presuppose pre-Islamic cosmological ideas, but it incorporates some of them in the cosmological aspects of its teaching.

It is also clear from the Qur'an, however, that not all the pagan Arabs were the same in outlook. Some at least among them believed in a supreme deity or 'high god'. For the most part they presented their petitions to the local deities, but in times of special stress they turned to the 'high god'; after the crisis had passed, however, they once more neglected the 'high god' [39.8/11; cf. 29.65]. From this belief in a supreme deity it was no doubt easy to pass to belief in God. The Qur'an, in calling on the people of Mecca to worship the Lord of the Ka'ba [106.3], may be assuming that many of the people of Mecca are in fact making this change. On the other hand, many Meccans, whether or not they acknowledged a supreme deity, certainly gave some worship to idols; these last are frequently attacked in the Qur'an, and referred to as the 'peers' or 'partners' (*andād, shurakā'*) ascribed to God by the pagans. Sometimes – no doubt in accordance with one strand in pre-Islamic thought – the pagan deities are treated as jinn (to be described presently); but at other items [53.23] they are spoken of as mere names of human origin. If the name is understood in the sense considered above, this statement means that, since the names of the deities are invented by men, who have *ex hypothesi* no knowledge of such realities except what has come to them by revelation, then the names do not correspond to anything in the real world.

Part of the old Arab cosmology was a belief in various types of spiritual beings, known collectively as jinn, with the singular *jinnī* which has been anglicized in translations of the *Arabian Nights* as 'genie'. It would appear that these were sometimes good spirits and sometimes bad. Part of sura 72 is connected with an occasion when jinn are said to have listened to Muhammad reciting the Qur'an and to have become Muslims, though others are destined for hell. Similar to the jinn, but superior to them and always good, are the angels. The Qur'an seems to presuppose familiarity with angels among the people addressed, and modern scholars mostly hold that the idea had come into Arabia from Jewish or Christian sources before the time of Muhammad. Acceptance of the idea was probably facilitated by the older Arab belief in jinn, and angels regarded as a type of jinn. In much the same way the concept of a *shaytān* or evil spirit seems to have been familiar to the Arabs before Muhammad, and to have come to them from Jewish and Christian sources.

There are traces in the Qur'an of the simple picture of the world presumably held by the pre-Islamic Arab of the desert. The earth is spread out like a carpet in a tent [91.6], while the heaven or sky is a roof or tent over it [21.32/3]. The sky is held up by God and so prevented from falling on the earth [22.65/4]. In a somewhat puzzling phrase mountains are said to have been thrown on the earth to keep it from shaking or swaying [16.15] – perhaps like heavy objects on a carpet in a gale. All this presumably comes from the nomadic Arab outlook. In other passages, however, God is spoken of as creating seven heavens [41.12/11]; and this idea must presumably have penetrated into Arabia from some region where Greek philosophy and science were familiar.

So much has been written about Jewish and Christian ideas present in the Qur'an that it will be sufficient here to insist that some cosmological ideas from Judaism, Christianity and Zoroastrianism were familiar to some pre-Islamic Arabs. This is only natural if one remembers the presence in Arabia of Jews and Christians, and the trade contacts of the Meccans with the Byzantine, Abyssinian and Persian empires. It is indeed clear from the stories of Muhammad's call to be a prophet that he was helped to interpret his first experiences by persons like Waraqa (the cousin of Muhammad's wife Khadīja) who knew a little about the Judaeo-Christian conception of revelation. Their knowledge might be slight and vague, but it contributed to Muhammad's understanding of his special vocation. It is noteworthy, however, that the word used first and most frequently is not the Judaeo-Christian word 'prophet' (*nabī*) but the distinctively Arabic word 'messenger' (*rasūl*). Not only this idea of the prophet or messenger came to the pre-Islamic Arabs from Jewish and Christian sources. Their cosmological ideas centring in the conception of God must also have been influenced; perhaps this influence encouraged the growth of the idea of the supreme god among the pre-Islamic Arabs. There may also have been Zoroastrian influence at the same points; but any distinctive Zoroastrian influence is most easily discerned in dualistic attitudes to good and evil, and the conception of the devil or Iblīs. The idea that Time is the source of good and evil may also have been affected by influences from Persia.

Along with these cosmological ideas one might mention the Arab conception of human society which is everywhere presupposed in the Qur'an. An essential feature of social structure in Arabia was the *qawm*, which presumably is best represented by 'tribe' in English, though it is often translated 'people'. The Arab would naturally imagine that the social structure with which he was familiar in the desert, and which continued after a fashion in towns like Mecca and Medina, was universal throughout the civilized world. So the Qur'an always speaks of a prophet or messenger being sent to a *qawm*. This social structure and the attitudes associated with it are presupposed in the Qur'anic stories of the prophets. Thus in the story of Joseph the brothers complain that, though they are an *'uṣba* – a kinship-group with a high degree of solidarity – their father does not treat them equally but prefers Joseph and his full brother [12.8]. At the same time, when persuading their father to allow Joseph to go with them [12.14], they argue that, since they are an *'uṣba*, they will all be adversely affected should a wolf eat Joseph. One suspects that the great men of Mecca made use of traditional ideas when it suited their personal ends. Again, the conception of *ijāra*, the giving of 'neighbourly protection', is applied metaphorically to God [46.31/0; 67.28; 72.22]; so strange is this conception to Europeans that the double reference to the practice in 23.88/90 – 'he gives protection, but none gives protection against him' – is often inadequately rendered.

39

4. The Historical Ideas Presupposed

Besides their general ideas about the structure of society the pre-Islamic Arabs had certain ideas about the distant and more recent past which might be labelled 'historical'. Their conception of the course of events in the past was linked with the social structure familiar to them. They had experience of the way in which a tribe would rise to a position of strength and prosperity, and then after a time decline and perhaps disappear. The Qur'an treats the disappearance of former tribes as a fact well-known to the Meccans, and interprets this fact as due to God's punishment for disobedience. Thus there is no conception of a course or movement of history along a single line, as it were. There is only the rise and fall of numerous tribes or peoples, with each of which various incidents are connected. Among the pre-Islamic Arabs there can have been little idea of the chronological relation of the different tribes or incidents; there was no frame of reference into which unconnected events could be fitted. Within each tribe there would be some knowledge of the succession of chiefs or leaders, and battles between tribes would give some points of contact between separate cycles of events. On the whole, however, history was conceived as the rise and fall of tribes and peoples, and for the most part each group was unconnected with the others.

Those who first heard the Qur'an were presumed to have a knowledge of the former existence of the tribes of 'Ād and Thamūd, to whom the prophets Hūd and Ṣāliḥ had been sent. In 34.16/15 the words 'the flood of the dam' are taken to refer to the bursting of the dam of Ma'rib in the Yemen. This event was remembered in Arab tradition as having led to the departure of various tribes from that region and their abandonment of an agricultural life for a nomadic one. At least two inscriptions recording a break-down of the irrigation system have been found by archaeologists, and it is now realized that the bursting of the dam symbolizes a stage in the decline of South Arabian civilization. Here, then, the Qur'an is referring to an event known to Muhammad's contemporaries by a genuine oral tradition. Much the same is true of a more recent event connected with 'the men of the elephant' [105.1] – an expedition from South Arabia with an elephant which reached the neighbourhood of Mecca but turned back without inflicting any damage. In thus insisting that there was a historical tradition about these and other events in Mecca, it is not claimed that those familiar with the events interpreted them in a theistic way. It may well be that this was an element of novelty contributed by the Qur'an; but that is a topic for the next chapter.

Besides this local tradition about events in Arabia there was some knowledge of certain parts of the historical sections of the Bible. This doubtless came through the same channels as the cosmological ideas. Even in the earlier suras of the Qur'an there are references to Biblical stories; but these references are not a detailed retelling of the story but are allusive in form, from which it may be inferred that there was some knowledge of the story among the hearers. The limitations of this inference, however, must be carefully noted. It does not mean that all Meccans knew all the Biblical stories perfectly, but only that some Meccans – perhaps only one or two at first – had a rough idea of the stories connected with the various names. After the Qur'an began to make allusions to the stories, however, the interest of both the Muslims and their opponents would be engaged. If they met someone who knew the stories, they would question him about the details; and they might even seek out those who could give them fuller information. The Muslims (including Muhammad) would want to understand the Qur'an better, whereas the opponents would be looking for points to criticize. Altogether acquaintance with the Biblical stories would be increasing in Mecca and Medina while Muhammad was there; and it would be natural to expect that this growing knowledge would be reflected in the Qur'an.

The kind of knowledge which the Qur'an presupposes in the people addressed is such as must have come to them orally. There is nothing to suggest that, even among the Jews of Medina, there was any scholarly knowledge of the Bible such as might have been obtained by reading. A few people may have been able to read, and may have read some of the Old and New Testaments; but, if so, they did not greatly influence the form of the stories handed on orally. In many cases the story as told or alluded to in the Qur'an resembles not that in the Bible itself, but a variant found in secondary works. Some Old Testament stories have a form similar to that in the Jewish

ISLAMIC REVELATION

explanatory amplifications of the Old Testament known as midrash; and the story of the miracle of the clay birds [3.49/3] is not from the canonical Gospels of the New Testament, but from a heretical Gnostic document. That stories of this character should have been current among ordinary people in Arabia is not surprising, but exactly what might be expected, since these stories and versions were current elsewhere among ordinary people. It is surely not in any way derogatory to suggest that the Qur'an gave its message not merely in the Arabic language, but in terms of the ideas familiar to the Arabs, not excluding those just mentioned.

It would also seem to be the case that in the earlier years of Muhammad's mission at Mecca his followers and the other Meccans, though they knew a little of some Biblical stories, treated these as disconnected incidents, in much the same way as they treated events in Arabian history. They probably were unaware of the chronological scheme of the Old and New Testaments, and of the temporal relations of the 'prophets' to one another. As the Muslims' general knowledge of Biblical material increased, so they would come to know more about the sequence of events and of personalities. The Qur'an has some chronological indications in passages from the later Meccan and Medinan periods. These considerations offer a way of dealing with the difficulty in the words 'O sister of Aaron' addressed to Mary the mother of Jesus [19.28/9], apparently confusing her with Miriam the sister of Moses and Aaron. Muslim scholars have several ingenious solutions of the difficulty, some of which are not altogether impossible. Perhaps it would be simpler, however, to admit that, since both names are rendered 'Maryam' in Arabic, the two women were in fact confused by ordinary people in Mecca who had no idea of Biblical chronology; the Qur'an then addressed these persons in terms of the ideas they had, including this misconception, since the communicating of the essential religious message would have been hindered rather than advanced by an attempt to correct this misconception.

In the third place, in addition to knowledge of the past history of Arabia and some of the historical sections of the Bible, the Qur'an presupposes knowledge of contemporary history. Obviously Muhammad's followers must have been

42

aware of what was going on around them, and of the events in which they themselves took part. At an early date there are references to the prosperity of the Meccans and their caravans. During the Medinan period there were many events which the Qur'an had to interpret for the Muslims. They did not require to be told *what* had happened, since they already knew that. Frequently, however, they needed to know *why* certain things had happened – the setback at Uḥud, for example – and what the significance of these things was in the purposes of God.

The purpose of this chapter has been to emphasize that communication does not take place in an intellectual vacuum, but presupposes a complex intellectual life in the recipients of the communication. The description of the intellectual life and the mentality of the pre-Islamic Arabs and the early Muslims has been illustrative rather than exhaustive. Some readers may want to omit some of the points made or to add others; and they may well be right. Even with such alterations of detail, however, the chapter will have served its purpose if it has shown that 'an Arabic Qur'an' presupposes a complex Arab intellectual life.

FOUR

NOVELTY IN THE CONTENT
OF THE QUR'AN

꙳

1. Its Relevance to the Contemporary Situation

It was fashionable at the beginning of the twentieth century to present the Qur'an as a selection of ideas from Judaism and Christianity with little distinctive merit and no novelty or originality. Such a view is a belated survival from the war-propaganda of the crusading period when Western Europe, in great fear of Muslim armies, had to embody its defensive attitudes in a falsified picture of Islam. When one considers the view out of context, merely by comparing the Qur'an with the Bible, there seems to be much to be said for it. This, however, is to assume that Muhammad made his proclamations in a vacuum. When one looks at both scriptures in their historical context, the matter takes on a different complexion. The Old Testament prophet did not speak in an intellectual vacuum any more than did Muhammad, but spoke to people familiar with the messages of previous prophets and with something of the past religious history of their people. This religious situation was presupposed. The novel and original message of each prophet assumed familiarity with many ideas, was expressed in terms of these ideas, and dealt with contemporary problems.

In *Muhammad at Mecca* I have attempted to show how the message of the earliest passages of the Qur'an was adapted to the situation in Mecca when Muhammad began his mission there.[1] It will thus be sufficient here to summarize what has already been argued in some detail. Among the passages generally agreed to be early those were selected in which opposition to Muhammad was neither expressly stated nor implied. In these passages five main points appeared to be insisted on: (1) God is all-powerful and good; (2) men will appear before

44

God on the Last Day to be judged and assigned to heaven or hell according to their deeds; (3) man ought to be grateful to God and worship him; (4) man should be generous with his wealth and upright; (5) Muhammad has been sent as a warner to bring this message from God to his fellows. Now the first four of these points might be said to be derived from Judaism or Christianity, though there are some differences of emphasis; for example, the older religions usually lay far less emphasis on generosity with wealth. The pivot of the new religious movement, however, was the fifth point; and, though the idea of conveying a divine message may be derived, the assertion that in particular Muhammad is such a messenger cannot be derived. Here at least is one element of originality.

Even the other ideas, however, when looked at in their historical context, are seen to be specially relevant to Mecca at that period. Mecca was a prosperous commercial centre whose caravans went as far as Damascus in the north and the Yemen in the south. Some of its trading enterprises had even wider ramifications. The great merchants were very wealthy men, and had come to believe that almost anything could be achieved by finance and careful planning. Besides this they were so engrossed in making money that they neglected the traditional duties falling upon them as clan leaders of looking after the poorer members of the clan. There had been a breakdown of the traditional desert morality with its insistence on most of the virtues essential to life in society. Only those aspects of morality connected with the *lex talionis* were still in force.

Now the five points listed are all relevant to this situation. To counteract the exaggerated views of human power and the failure to recognize its limitations men are called upon to acknowledge God's power, to be grateful to him and to worship him. To counteract the breakdown of traditional morality and the failure of the traditional sanctions to deal with this, it is insisted that a man's ultimate fate depends on the Last Judgement, and the basis of this is the man's conduct as an individual. Thus a sanction for morality is provided which is suited to the individualistic outlook of the great merchants. To counter the close-fistedness of the merchants with their wealth and their neglect of the needy of their kin, it is insisted that in the Judgement an important question will be whether the man was niggardly or generous with his wealth. Thus, in respect of the first four points, even if the Qur'an is presenting old ideas, it is selecting and emphasizing aspects which were specially relevant to the Mecca of the early seventh century.

The fifth point – that Muhammad has been sent as a messenger and warner to his people – is in part an assertion of the special application of the message to Muhammad's environment. The Qur'an itself acknowledges that its message is in essentials a repetition of that to which the earlier monotheistic religions are a response; but this message has been freshly revealed to Muhammad. Yet as the conception of revelation and the first recipient of revelation is developed in the Qur'an it comes to have several elements of originality. Because a large part of the message is the proclamation that wrongdoers and unbelievers will be punished, both eschatologically and temporally, Muhammad is told in early passages to say that his function is that of a 'warner' and that he has no political ambitions. After the Hijra to Medina, however, the concept of 'messenger' – the commonest title for Muhammad as recipient of the revelation – is enlarged; besides communicating the divine messages it is his task to administer the community of Muslims in accordance with these messages. In this way a political role is, as it were, thrust upon him. The Old Testament prophet also had a political role, but 'the Messenger of God' came to have vastly greater responsibilities.

When one turns from the earliest passages of the Qur'an to later ones, it is clear that many of the regulations for the Muslim community of Medina are original at least in their details. The Muslim community grew and developed gradually, chiefly by adapting existing Arabian usages. Even the ideals which may be said to have guided the process of adaptation, though in a sense shared by other peoples, had a special Arabian flavour. It is hardly necessary, however, to examine these matters at length. It will be more instructive to look at the development of the Qur'anic attitude to pre-Islamic Arabian religion.

It is noteworthy that in the earliest passages of the Qur'an there is no attack on the existing religion. The five points are positive, except that punishment is threatened for niggardliness and for unbelief in God and the Last Judgement. The verse calling on the Meccans to worship the Lord of the Ka'ba

[106.3] seems to hope that existing believers in a supreme deity (with other lesser ones) will see in the Qur'anic proclamations a purified version of what they already believe. In other words the Qur'an may be said to envisage a smooth transition from the higher forms of the existing religion to the new religion; that is to say, the emphasis is on amplifying and adding to existing beliefs, not on discarding old ones, though it may have been hoped that old beliefs incompatible with the new beliefs would in due course fade away. The change of direction (if this metaphor be allowed to pass for the moment) came about with bitter Qur'anic attacks on the polytheistic aspects of the existing religion. This presumably followed on the appearance of vigorous opposition to Muhammad's movement, and this opposition – no doubt for complex reasons – was linked with some resurgence of idol-worship. Thus Islam has come to be noted for its insistence that God is one and that there are no other beings to whom worship may properly be offered.

In describing this development it is impossible to avoid anthropomorphic metaphors, and to say, according to the form of words adopted in this study, that the Qur'an 'hoped' and 'changed its direction or policy'. It must be insisted that this is not a mere verbal trick to avoid saying that Muhammad hoped or changed his policy. To anticipate some of the discussions of Chapter 9, it might be suggested to the European reader that he think of the Qur'an as proceeding from some kind of social force operative in the community as a whole. This would be something beyond Muhammad's consciousness, though working through him. The observer sees that this force, as it directs the society towards a more satisfactory condition, will naturally first explore the direct road forwards, that is, to build a new order of society on a modified form of existing beliefs. In course of time it becomes clear that other social forces resistant to change are linked with aspects of the old beliefs. In order to weaken these forces and allow the social reform to proceed it was necessary to have a criterion to distinguish between the supporters of reform and those who wanted to retain the *status quo*. The social force behind the reform produced this criterion by its new 'policy' of attacking the polytheistic aspects of the old beliefs.

47

Despite the bitterness of the attack on idols much of the old religion was absorbed into Islam. Conceptions which are shared with Judaism and Christianity come in the Qur'an to have a distinctive Arabian form. There is less emphasis on God's creation of the world and of man in the distant past and more on his all-embracing activity in the world at the present time. Although he is the merciful and compassionate, he comes to have some of the inscrutability ascribed by the pre-Islamic Arabs to Time. There are many passages about God's control of the whole process of human birth; and one wonders whether in this he has taken over some of the attributes of the old Arabian and Semitic deities who were identified with male and female creative powers. Thus both in the Qur'an's rejection of Arabian polytheism and in its implicit acceptance of features of the old Arabian religion, there is something not derived from Judaism or Christianity and to be reckoned original.

This relationship of Islam to the old Arabian religion is paralleled by the relationship of Old Testament religion to the old Canaanite religion. There is the same fierce denunciation of aspects of polytheism. At the same time animal sacrifice, which really belonged to Canaanite religion, and was closely linked with the ideas of that religion, came to have an important place in the worship of the Israelites. Indeed, in so far as Christianity is the consummation of the Old Testament, sacrifice may be said to have become central, since the crucifixion of Jesus was interpreted both by himself and by his followers in terms of sacrifice.[2] The parallelism in this matter between Islam and the Old Testament religion is no accident, but is rather something which is implicit in a true monotheism.

This examination, then, of the relation of the Qur'an to the Meccan and Arabian environment has made it clear that the message is specially suited to the needs of the people among whom Muhammad lived, and is not a mere repetition of older ideas. If the Qur'an contains truths that are in some sense eternal, yet they have been adapted to the particular milieu. Or perhaps, in the light of the later spread of Islam it would be better to say that the particular message conveyed to the people of Mecca and Medina had from the first implicit in it aspects of universality.

2. The Interpretation of Contemporary Events

One of the functions of the religious leader of the prophetic type is to show his people how their faith is confirmed by events which happen to them, and how certain other events, which might seem to destroy that faith, need not be interpreted in such a way. Before looking at some of the Qur'anic interpretations it will be useful to look at an Old Testament instance. The incidents in the story of the 'sin of Achan' (*Joshua*, 7) are selected for this purpose, partly because the story is nowadays unfamiliar, partly because the matter is relatively unimportant (and unlikely to raise theological passions), and partly because the element of the supernatural is at a minimum. There are also some parallels to the situation of the Muslims after the battle of Uḥud.

The incidents took place shortly after the entry of the Israelites into Palestine across the Jordan and their capture of the city of Jericho. They were filled with elation at their success. When it came to attacking a small place called Ai, which lay in their line of advance, they were so confident that they thought it unnecessary for the whole army to attack Ai, and sent a relatively small force of three thousand men. To their consternation this force was put to flight. Joshua in deep despair spent the whole day in prayer prostrate on his face before the ark of God, and eventually was told by God that the discomfiture was due to the fact that the people had sinned. Next day lots were drawn and the lot fell upon Achan. He confessed that he had taken a rich robe, some silver and a wedge of gold from the spoils of Jericho, although this had been forbidden by Joshua. Thereupon he, his family, his domestic animals and all his material possessions were taken apart, and killed and destroyed by stoning and burning. The attack on Ai was renewed and was successful; but it may be noted that thirty thousand men were placed in an ambush while the rest of the army made a frontal attack.

The important point in this story is that, once the rout before Ai had taken place, it was necessary to restore confidence by showing that it was not due to military inferiority but to something else, namely, sin or disobedience. According to the ideas of primitive religion this sin was felt to be a pollution or infection of the whole body; but the steps taken led to the effective cleansing of the whole body. The modern historian may be inclined to ask some questions. He will want to know whether the lot was manipulated, or whether nearly everybody had in fact taken something. The latter may well have been the case, for it is nowhere stated that no other spoils had been taken privately. The phrase in verse 26 that 'the Lord turned from the fierceness of his anger' could mean that there were no further polluting articles in the camp; but it could also mean that Achan and his goods were taken as representing all sinful men and wrongfully-taken spoils, so that their removal entailed the complete removal of the pollution. The modern historian might rather say that the defeat was due to the fact that most of the army was thinking chiefly of the spoil, while the punishment of Achan helped to curb any undue desire for self-enrichment.

Though there can be no question of imitation, there is a parallel between the inspired interpretation of the rout at Ai in the Old Testament and that of the reverse at Uḥud in the Qur'an. The Muslims were greatly elated after their victory at Badr, and were therefore correspondingly depressed after Uḥud. From a military point of view Uḥud was not a serious reverse; the Meccans had still failed to take even one life for each life lost, although they had sworn they would take several. The difficulty was that the Muslims had taken Badr as a sign that God was fighting for them, and this had become the basis of their confidence. After Uḥud they began to doubt if God was really fighting for them, and their confidence ebbed away. The Qur'an dealt with this loss of confidence by showing that the reverse was due, not to any change on God's part, but to the disobedience of the archers who left their posts because they were eager for plunder. This interpretation and Muhammad's own steadiness in the crisis led in due course to the Muslims regaining confidence.

The Qur'an is constantly interpreting contemporary events and situations. Early in the Meccan period it asserts or implies that Meccan commercial prosperity is due to God. The theistic interpretation of earlier events like the expedition of the elephant and the destruction of various peoples was probably first made in the Qur'an, but it is conceivable that interpretations along similar lines were already current among the Arabs. For most of the Meccan period the Muslims could not but be aware of the opposition to their religious movement, and this no doubt made them wonder why, if Muhammad was really sent by God, he should yet have to meet such opposition. The Qur'an asserts again and again that it was common and indeed normal for a 'messenger' to meet such opposition, and cited many Biblical and Arabian instances. Eventually the messenger was saved, despite the opposition, even when the whole community was destroyed. Against this background it was to be expected that the Qur'an would interpret the victory at Badr as a punishment of the Meccans for disbelieving the message, and a vindication of Muhammad's claim to be a messenger.

Another aspect of the contemporary situation where the Qur'anic interpretation was important was the relationship of the Muslims to the established communities of Jews and Christians with which they were in contact. One of the factors in this situation was the recognition by Islam of the essential identity of its message with that of Judaism and Christianity. Another factor was the criticism of Muhammad and the Qur'an by the Jews of Medina. In so far as a Muslim was able to appreciate the criticisms, they were likely to make him doubt the genuineness of the Qur'an and of Muhammad's claim to be a messenger. The behaviour of the Jews was thus a serious threat to the growing community of Muslims. Difficulties with Christians came chiefly towards the end of Muhammad's life when Christian tribes opposed the Islamic advance northwards in the direction of Syria.

One of the points in the Qur'anic interpretation of this situation was that the Jews opposed Muhammad and criticized him because they themselves had deviated from the original pure form of their own religion; and the same came to be said also of the Christians. It was not surprising, then, that they rejected the Qur'an, since it basically repeated the pure religion and not the corruptions of the Jews and Christians. This pure religion was further identified with the religion of Abraham, and it was insisted that he was neither a Jew nor a Christian. This last point, of course, is quite correct, since a Jew may be defined either as a descendant of Jacob (also called Israel) or as an adherent of the religious community based on the revelation to Moses; and both Jacob and Moses are descendants of Abraham. The Qur'an connects Abraham and Ishmael with Mecca, but does not speak of any Arabs as descended from Ishmael, though later Muslims accepted the Old Testament genealogies on this matter. There was a certain fitness in the claim that Islam was a restoration of the religion of Abraham in its purity; in this way Muslims were protected from the intellectual attacks of Jews and Christians, and yet the relationship to the two older religions was maintained. In its original form the claim approved itself to people who had no knowledge of the Jewish and Christian scriptures; later when Muslim scholars had gained some knowledge of the Bible and were meeting people familiar with it they had to elaborate further the theory of 'the corruption of the scriptures'.

From all this it will be clear that the Qur'anic interpretation of contemporary events and situations was no academic exercise, but was practical guidance for the community in the handling of actual problems. The guidance was no mere mechanical application of some rule, but was a creative response to the particular challenge. There can be no question but that in these matters the Qur'an shows originality.

3. The Qur'anic Claims to Novelty

There are thus good grounds for holding that the Qur'an is no mere repetition of Jewish and Christian ideas, but has elements of novelty and originality. The common Muslim view of the Qur'an, however, implies a further claim to novelty which most European scholars find it difficult to admit. Muslims regard the statements of the Qur'an about the distant past – for example, about Biblical times – as more authoritative than the normal historical tradition. This is in fact a claim that the Qur'an is an independent source of historical information. Now the modern scholar looks on the Qur'an as an important source of information for contemporary events, but in respect of the distant past is not prepared to admit that it does more than reflect the historical ideas current in Mecca. The point at which this question is most urgent is in respect of the Islamic belief, based on the Qur'an, that Jesus did not die on the cross. The first question to be investigated here, then, is whether the Qur'an itself actually makes a claim of this kind, or whether the claim depends rather on later interpretations of the Qur'an. The investigation may begin with the verse [11.49/31]:

> That is from the accounts of the unseen which we
> reveal to you (Muhammad); neither you nor your people
> knew it before this . . .

This comes at the end of a version of the story of Noah which includes God's refusal to help Noah's unbelieving son. The wording requires us to hold that in this case the Qur'an is *not* referring to a story commonly known to the Meccans. The matter is not so simple, however, if two other passages are considered where the same phrase occurs: 'from the accounts of the unseen which we reveal to you (Muhammad)' (*min anbā' al-ghayb nūḥī-hā ilay-ka*). In both cases what is emphasized is not Muhammad's ignorance of the story, but his absence from the actual events. In the story of Zacharias and Mary it is said 'you (Muhammad) were not with them when they threw their pens (to decide) which of them should take charge of Mary, and you were not with them when they were quarreling' [3.44/39]. Similarly at the end of the story of Joseph it is stated: 'you (Muhammad) were not with them when they were plotting and agreed on a plan' [12.102/3].

Now it has to be admitted that there is no inherent philological difficulty in taking all these verses to mean that the Qur'an has been conveying factual historical information which was previously unknown at least to most of the hearers. It would seem, however, that the verses in question can also be understood in a slightly different way. The early revelation, 96.4, 5, may be kept in mind, interpreting it to mean that God 'by the pen taught man what he did not know', that is, in the scriptures gave man accounts of what had happened in the distant past. This seems to express the wonder of men from an oral culture when they discover how through writing they can have a close contact with the past. Something of the same wonder is present in the two later passages about 'accounts of the unseen', especially when one remembers that the word translated 'unseen', *ghayb*, need mean no more than something at which one is not present. There is therefore some justification for holding that in the first passage the emphasis is on the absence of information by the usual channel of oral tradition;

and this would leave open the possibility that there had been some information received by the – to the Arabs – extraordinary channel of written books.

It would thus seem not impossible to hold that Muhammad had received some knowledge of these stories, previously unknown to him, from an informant who had gained his knowledge from books. The existence of such an informant is not denied in the Qur'an in reply to charges made by the Meccans [16.103/5]; it is insisted that he could not have produced the actual text since his speech is foreign. The view being suggested here is in accordance with this reply; although Muhammad knew the stories from his informant, the Qur'anic text would come to him as all other Qur'anic texts came, and the message of the Qur'an would presuppose at least his own familiarity with the story, though its essence would be the 'lesson' of the story. Such a view receives strong support from the last verse in the sura of Joseph [12.111]:

> In telling the story of these (people) there was indeed
> a lesson for men of insight; it was not an invented tale,
> but the confirmation of what (revelation) was present
> already, and the exposition of everything, and guidance
> and a mercy to a believing people.

It may be argued from this passage that, since the Qur'an is the confirmation of previous revelation, its stories must have been present in that revelation. Certainly the Qur'an does not claim to give information hitherto unknown to any living human being; and those who interpret it as making such a claim seem to be guilty of innovation. The view suggested here – that it is only the form and the 'lesson' of the stories which comes by revelation – is well grounded in itself, and has the added attraction of being compatible with a 'modern' account of revelation.

On the basis of this result the passage about the crucifixion may now be looked at briefly. It occurs in a recital of various misdeeds of the Jews; these include:

> ... their saying, We killed the Messiah, Jesus son of
> Mary, the messenger of God; yet they did not kill him
> and did not crucify him, but it was made to seem to

them (that they did so); those who differ in regard to
him are in doubt about him; they have of him no knowledge but only follow opinion; they certainly did not
kill him; on the contrary God raised him to himself;
God is almighty, wise [4.157/6 f.].

The first thing to notice is that this passage is not an attack on
Christianity, but a defence of Christianity against the Jews.
The Jewish claim that they had killed the Messiah – for the
Qur'an 'the Messiah' (al-Masīḥ) is a name or title whose
significance is unknown – is more than a bare statement of
fact; it implies a claim to have somehow shown Christianity
to be false. It is this implied claim which the Qur'an is concerned
to deny. Since it regards Jesus as a prophet or messenger of
God, it is unthinkable that his work should have been frust-
rated. The Qur'an gives expression to this belief, which must
have had deep roots in the Arab mentality of the day.

The belief that the upright man must ultimately prosper in
this life is one strand of thought in the Old Testament; e.g. 'I
have been young and now am old; yet have I not seen the
righteous forsaken nor his seed begging bread' (Psalm 37.25).
Even when the question is raised, as in the Book of Job,
whether suffering is always the result of sin, the upright man
(Job) is made to prosper in the end. The Christian, of course,
believes that the crucifixion is a victory and not a defeat because
it is followed by the resurrection of Jesus and birth of the
Church. The Qur'an, being addressed to people who had a
deep conviction that the career of a messenger of God could
not end in outward defeat, denied the Jewish claim and added
the vague words 'it was made to seem to them' or 'a resemblance was made for them'. Some such statement as this was presumably the only way in which, in this Arabian environment,
the Jewish claim to have defeated a messenger of God could be
rebutted. In later times Muslim scholars interpreted the phrase
in terms of Gnostic (heretical) accounts of the crucifixion and
victory of Jesus; and there may already have been some vague
knowledge of this among Muhammad's contemporaries.
Essentially, then, in this passage the Qur'an is asserting in the
thought-forms of the Arabian environment a spiritual truth
acceptable to Christians, namely, that the culmination of the

career of Jesus was a victory for him and not for the Jews. The validity of this 'lesson' of the Qur'an may be maintained – indeed is better maintained – without claiming that it is a source of historical information about the first century A.D.

It may be indicated before passing on that, provided there is an eirenic relationship between Muslims and Christians, this passage is not an insuperable obstacle. Remembering the verse (2 *Samuel*, 12.9) where it is stated that David killed Uriah with the sword of the Ammonites, one might suggest asking the question, 'Who killed Jesus?'; and the answer could be that it was not the Jews and not the Romans, but he himself, in the sense that he accepted his death and indeed that his was the dominant will in the whole process; so it 'was only made to seem' to the Jews that they did so.

FIVE

THE RECEIVING OF REVELATION

☻

1. The Response to Prophets

Several of the stories in the Qur'an suggest that the response of a community to a messenger who comes to them from God is little more than a single act of acceptance or rejection. Thus in sura 26, verses 105-91, there is a series of stories parallel to one another dealing with Noah, Hūd, Ṣāliḥ, Lot and Shu'ayb. In each of these stories the messenger in effect says 'I am God's messenger to you; fear him, and do as I say; otherwise there is a punishment in store for you'. This is all in accordance with the conception of the messenger as a warner. As the stories are told in sura 26 nothing is said about reasons for accepting the message which the warner brings. It is as if the messenger speaks with sufficient authority in himself. It may be, however, that the stories are simplified at this point in sura 26 because the interest there is in another aspect.

The use of the word *ghāfilūn*, 'negligent, inattentive', is also important in this connection. It is often linked with a mention of God's 'signs' [as in 10.7, 92]. Now many of the earlier passages of the Qur'an were a recitation of the signs in nature of God's power and goodness. These phenomena were always present for men to observe, but most men had been 'negligent', that is, had not noticed the phenomena nor been aware of their significance until their attention was called to them by the revelations. In this way those who respond positively to the Qur'an receive enlightenment and a fuller understanding of the world. It seems to be implied in some passages, however, that men might be expected to understand the import of some signs without any explicit revelation; to the extent that they have failed to understand, it may be said that they have not been paying attention to the signs and have therefore been 'negligent'. When men respond positively to the revelation, they cease to be 'negligent' and become instead believers.

There is a certain mystery about the particular response a man makes. It is not clear why some men respond positively and others negatively. In the Qur'an God is presented as being in supreme control of the universe, and thus the positive or negative response is in some sense due to him. One passage [2.6/5 f.] describes persons from whom Muhammad had experienced invincible hostility:

> For those who disbelieved it is the same whether you
> warn them or not, they will not believe; God has set
> a seal on their hearts, and over their hearing and their
> eyes is a cover . . .

Other phrases used are that God 'guides' men and 'leads them astray' (*hadā, aḍalla*). Sometimes the phrases are used absolutely, as complete descriptions of God's activity. The guidance may be achieved, however, by 'enlarging a man's breast for Islam' (*yashraḥ ṣadra-hu*), and the leading astray by making his breast 'narrow' (*ḍayyiq*) [6.125]. In other passages there is mention of God's help or succour (*naṣr, tawfīq*) or contrariwise his abandonment (*khidhlān*). Whatever the words used, there is an element of inscrutability in whether a man's response is positive or negative.

The simplified description of the response to a messenger belongs in the main to the Meccan period. After the Hijra to Medina the process of revelation and response became more complicated. To the first revelations at Mecca both Muhammad himself and several other men made a positive response. These believers came in time to form a group with some life of its own as a group. The Hijra led to the inclusion of far more persons in the group of believers, so that it was now a community. The believers were also dominant politically in the oasis of Medina. To this group or community of believers there came further revelations to guide them in many aspects of the common life in which all the inhabitants of the oasis participated. The *qawm* or 'people' to whom Muhammad was sent had thus become a complex socio-political entity. It had grown out of the first responses to revelation, but it had developed through later responses to later revelations in which the existence of the community of believers was presupposed. It is thus appropriate to speak of the 'whole organism of historical Islam' as having come into existence here. In this organism the Qur'an plays an important function.

Even those whose response to the messenger is negative continue to have a relationship with the revelation. In the terminology suggested in Chapter 1 they belong to the ecto-soma of the revelation. In practical terms this means that they continue to be influenced by the ideas present in the revelation and also by the group of persons who have responded positively. They do not necessarily accept the ideas or have friendly relations with the Muslims; but even where there is vigorous rejection of the ideas and active hostility to the persons, the influence is still in a sense present. Moreover the unbelievers continued to be addressed in the Qur'an, and Muhammad was instructed how to reply to their objections. In this way there was a continuing and developing relationship even between the unbelievers and the revelation.

In a slightly different position are the groups at Medina known as 'those in whose hearts is disease' and 'the hypocrites'. These were persons who had at least nominally accepted Islam at the time of the Hijra, but had then become dissatisfied with the new circumstances in Medina, and were opposed to Muhammad for mainly political reasons. They thus belonged to the endosoma, but were trying to break away from it. Their response to the message might be said to be religiously positive but otherwise negative.

2. Grounds for Accepting the Revelation

In the Old Testament the idea is to be found that a prophet or divine message is authenticated by the occurrence of a 'sign', understood as a paranormal event. Thus when God sends Moses to the Israelites, Moses is afraid that they will not believe him; and God thereupon gives him two 'signs' [*Exodus*, 4.1-9], the turning of his rod into a serpent and back again, and the inducement of leprosy on his hand and its removal; if these signs do not convince the Israelites he is to pour water on the ground and it will become blood. Another instance is when the prophet Isaiah is sent to King Hezekiah to inform him of a paranormal event which is to occur as a sign [*Isaiah*, 38.4-8], namely, the shadow on the sundial moving backwards.

This conception of the authenticating or validating sign is prominent in later Islamic theology. In the Qur'an, however, there is little trace of it except in connection with the story of Moses. The signs of the rod-serpent and the leprous hand are mentioned more than once; e.g. in 7.103/1-118/5; 26.30/29-26.45/4. It is to be noted, however, that these signs are not used to convince the Israelites but only Pharaoh [as in *Exodus*, 7]. So far as Muhammad himself is concerned, he does not appear to have used any signs of this kind to convince the Arabs that he was a messenger. The 'signs' of which there is frequent mention in the earlier suras are to convince men of God's goodness and power, not of the genuineness of Muhammad's mission. Again, in so far as Muhammad was a 'warner' of punishment for not believing in God and his signs, the battle of Badr could be regarded as a prediction come true, and therefore as a proof of Muhammad's messengership. This thought is not absent from the Qur'an, for the victory of Badr is regarded as the punishment of the Meccans and a confirmation of all Muhammad's claims; but there is nowhere any special emphasis on it as validating his position as messenger. The success of Badr had gone to the heads of the Muslims, and it was probably unnecessary to insist on its character as a validation, since the Muslims already believed this.

The Qur'an appears to envisage two main grounds of this kind for accepting the revelation. Firstly, it expects men to respond positively to the depth of conviction in Muhammad and his known uprightness of character. These factors, in conjunction with his complete self-confidence, doubtless led many men to the acceptance of his message. Secondly, it would seem that the Qur'an was regarded as in some way through its literary form self-authenticating. This point is implicit in the challenges to produce a sura or ten suras like it [10.38/9; 11.13/16]. Later it was discussed whether the inimitability of the Qur'an was in respect of its contents or of its literary form and style. Modern readers would agree that the contents are such that no Arab of the time was capable of effectively imitating them. Muslim scholarship on the whole, however, has thought

chiefly of the inimitability of the literary qualities. The underlying belief is that, since there is something superhuman
about the Qur'an in its literary aspect, it cannot be a human
production, and therefore is, as it claims, the speech of
God. The miraculous character of the Qur'an was enhanced
by the assertion (for dubious reasons) that Muhammad was
illiterate.

If it could be proved that the Qur'an was a genuine independent source of information about events in the distant past, this
would strengthen in the eyes of some people its claim to be of
divine origin. Grounds have been given already, however, for
thinking that the Qur'an itself does not make such a claim. It
should be noted, too, that a claim to know that X happened can
only be verified if at some later date normal historical reasons
are found for holding that this was the case. Certainly there is
no suggestion that anyone accepted the Qur'anic message
because of such a belief.

So far the grounds for accepting the Qur'an that have been considered have all been conscious grounds. The modern conception of man, however, assigns a large place to the unconscious. When the modern historian speaks of the social and
economic factors underlying some movement in the past, he is
mostly thinking of unconscious grounds. The person acting
may sometimes be partly aware of these factors, but often he is
unaware. It is above all the observer – either the contemporary
non-participant or the later historian – who sees the social and
economic aspects of the events, and forms theories about their
influence on the historical process. It is not necessary in the
present study to do more than indicate the existence of grounds
of this type for accepting or rejecting the revelation. The
Meccan situation has been analysed in detail in *Muhammad at
Mecca* and also in the first section of the previous chapter here;
and the relation of such factors to men's conscious ideas is
examined in *Islam and the Integration of Society* and *Truth in
the Religions*.

3. The Arabic Conception of Knowledge

The nature of the response to the Qur'an, at least in the first
century or so of Islam, and the precise character of its place

and function in the life of the Islamic community, are partly conditioned by the distinctive conception of knowledge current among the Arabs in the seventh century. The focus of an examination of this conception is the Arabic word *'ilm*. It is often translated 'science' nowadays, and used as the word 'science' is used in European languages. The traditional religious scholars, however, are still known as ulema (*'ulamā'*) – the noun of agent from this root – but it would be inappropriate to think of them as scientists. What is relevant to the present study, however, is not the total range of meanings of *'ilm*, but the distinctive meaning (or group of meanings) of this word in Arabic, which, even if it occurs in other languages in corresponding words, is not so prominent there.

This distinctive meaning of 'knowledge' in Arabic may provisionally be indicated by the English word 'wisdom'. It is wisdom in respect of the general conduct of human life. Further, it is looked upon as something which only very few persons possess in an eminent degree, persons who may be spoken of as 'sages' or 'men of wisdom'. Men other than this select few attain a measure of wisdom only in so far as they are able to 'enter into' the thoughts of the sages. The ordinary man or woman can add nothing to the human race's store of wisdom, but only the sage. Thus study, learning and the acquiring of knowledge come to be identified with the process of memorizing the words of the sages. Presumably the idea in this is that, if one memorizes the exact words in which wisdom is expressed, one will be able to meditate on these words continually; when some event happens to a man he will remember an appropriate saying; and so in general one will 'enter into' the wisdom of the sages. It is further implied here that the process of entering into wisdom is much more than simply understanding the literal or primary meaning of the text.

All this is in sharp opposition to a prominent aspect of the European conception of knowledge, namely, that indicated by the words 'knowledge as a source of power'. Scientific knowledge gives man power over nature, but knowledge of history and literature, in so far as they deepen one's understanding of human nature, give one power over men. Many persons, however, can contribute to the store of knowledge in this sense. The post-graduate student who writes a doctoral thesis is supposed to be able to make a slight addition to the sum of human knowledge. Even persons with less intellectual training may make a contribution – for example, by collecting particular facts about local birds or butterflies or plants or on matters of parochial history or archaeology. Such collections of facts are useful to better qualified persons in the framing of wide-ranging theories.

The conception of knowledge as a source of power has an important influence on the European attitude to the study of the religion and the secular history of other peoples. If the modern European has to engage in war against some Asian country, he will want to know a lot about its past, for he considers that such knowledge will enable him to forecast better the reaction of his enemy to various situations. Religion is an element in this knowledge. Sometimes the Christian missionary takes to strategic thinking of a military type, and considers that knowledge of other religions will assist him towards his goal of making converts. Islam, on the other hand, has mostly disdained any deep study of other religions. In so far as knowledge is wisdom, and in so far as other religions according to the Islamic view contain a large admixture of error, the Muslim is unlikely to gain wisdom by studying them, and may well infect himself with erroneous ideas. It is a common experience of Christian scholars of Islam that Muslims ask them why they devote so much energy to the study of Islam if they do not believe in it. In medieval times even the secular history of non-Muslim states and empires was neglected by Muslim historians, although they had access to information. In this sphere perhaps besides thinking of knowledge as wisdom they were influenced by the attitude of the Arab tribe to the 'boasting' or self-glorification of other tribes.

The contrast between the Arab and European conceptions of knowledge has here been stated in an extreme form, but it will at once be noticed that neither party is restricted to a single conception of knowledge. For the European the study of great literature would be held to give wisdom, even more than it gave knowledge of human nature. The European student is concerned with the actual words of Shakespeare or T. S. Eliot, which he memorizes to a slight extent, and, unless he is a bad student, is not content with abstract summaries of their thought.

Similarly traditional Islamic learning has included philosophical theology and even certain natural sciences to a limited extent, and in studying these its attitude has been closer to that of the Europeans than to one based on the conception of knowledge as wisdom. Nevertheless the broad distinction remains, and it is specially noteworthy when the whole system of modern European education is compared with the traditional Islamic system; the latter has to some extent remained in force up to the present time, though it is now being replaced in most Islamic countries by a system of the European type.

Because of the general Islamic attitude to 'wisdom' and 'men of wisdom', the transmission of knowledge in Islamic environments has taken a distinctive form. Memorization of the exact words of the sage has played a large part, whether it was the legendary pre-Islamic Luqmān or the early leaders of the Sufi movement. Very naturally Muhammad came to be regarded as a 'man of wisdom' and his sayings – technically known as 'Traditions' – were reverently treasured and handed on. The Traditions have become an important part of the intellectual heritage of Muslims. By about the year 800 Muslim scholars were realizing how easy it was to invent stories about Muhammad, for many people were doing it, while others were making slight changes in genuine stories. They therefore established criteria for deciding between true and false Traditions. Basically these criteria were the accuracy of the memory and the honesty of each transmitter; and the application of these criteria required that one should know the names of all the persons involved in the transmission of a particular anecdote from Muhammad down to the present time. Thus the Islamic world came to produce numerous biographical dictionaries of the scholars responsible for passing on the wisdom of the past.

The Qur'an, as divine wisdom, was treated similarly and with even greater reverence. There was the difference, however, that it had been written down officially about 650, though the form of writing used was one which left certain ambiguities; that is, at certain points the reader had to decide between two or more ways of reading a particular group of signs. The different sets of readings were for long memorized by the experts and handed on orally, so that what happened in this field was also in conformity with Islamic ideas about the transmission of wisdom. In the case of the Qur'an above all it seems to have been held that by memorization and repetition of the text a man would gradually enter into its wisdom. Sympathetic European observers have held that the constant repetition of the Qur'an has a subtle unconscious effect on the whole outlook of Muslims.

Once revelations have been written down or memorized as in the case of the Bible and the Qur'an, the response to them becomes continuous. It is not merely the first response of the first hearers that has to be considered, but that of later generations as they in turn make their response to the sacred texts. This has happened in Judaism and Christianity, but it has probably happened to a greater extent in Islam because of the conception of knowledge as wisdom. The revealed scripture thus becomes, as it were, the backbone of the organism of revelation. This metaphor, however, must not be pressed too far. Because the organism is alive, the function of the sacred text gradually changes. Even as it comes to later generations, it is slightly different from what it was previously, for it comes as part of a tradition in which the responses of previous generations are also included. The son who is taught the Qur'an by his father learns also in the process something of his father's responses to the Qur'an. Each generation comes to make its response to the Qur'an or other divine revelation conditioned by two factors: the whole history of the religious community up to that point; and the contemporary situation in which it itself has to act. It need not be emphasized that these two factors are different for each generation. If we consider only, say, 1935 and 1960, we see that the two factors were vastly different for the members of all the great religions.

Every great religious community, and many another community as well, has to make provision for the handing on to succeeding generations of its knowledge. In primitive times the father would often be the teacher, and the relation of teacher and pupil is often regarded as analogous to that of father and son. It has been noted that the Islamic tradition emphasizes the gifts of memory, but it also looked at a teacher's other qualities. These were tested by considering his freedom from heresy. In terms of the line of thought now being pursued this is a test of the adequacy of his responses to the sacred texts; and

E   65

so it is an implicit admission that he is transmitting not only texts but also responses and attitudes. The transmission of learning is thus an important part of the work of the community.[1]

The strength of the conception of wisdom as knowledge in Islam may be illustrated by noting the fate of a contrasting idea. Al-Ghazālī (d. 1111), a great Islamic theologian and mystic, worked out a theory by which many people of a mystical bent had a spiritual experience comparable to that of a prophet. The word he used was *dhawq*, which properly means 'taste' in the primary sense. His theory started from the difference between hearing a description of a place or person and actually seeing the place or meeting the person; and he argued that there was a similar difference between understanding the descriptions of spiritual realities in the Qur'an and Traditions and having a direct experience of them. This direct experience or 'taste' he maintained that mystics had. On the whole he does not seem to have claimed that this direct experience brought the mystics novel truths, but only that they had a fuller, because direct, knowledge of the truths of Qur'anic and Traditional wisdom. To most Europeans this seems a reasonable theory; yet it has to be recorded that despite al-Ghazālī's great authority this theory won little acceptance. Doubtless this was because the theory was not in accordance with the conception of knowledge as wisdom.

It may be thought strange that the Arab conception of knowledge as wisdom has spread far beyond the Arab world among Muslims of many races. The most obvious explanation of this fact is that, since the Qur'an deals with basic human problems, it is widely accepted. Where one is dealing with the basic realities of human life, and where the verbal message is supported by a welcoming community, as is the case with Islam, the categories implicit in language become irrelevant. People in danger of drowning accept any efficient rescuer. This, however, cannot be the complete explanation. When a body of people from a distinctive cultural background all become Muslims, there are bound to come times of stress and strain of one kind or another, and at such times their responses will be partly conditioned by their previous cultural background. Because they are Muslims they will normally think in Qur'anic terms as they respond to the tension; but the verses they select and the interpretation they give to these verses will be influenced by their previous culture. Such developments may lead to bitter disputes within the community, for each party may feel that the others are threatening something which it considers vital to the whole life of the community.

The problem here adumbrated is worthy of further study in respect of both Christianity and Islam. I have considered some aspects of it elsewhere,[2] but much remains to be done. The heart of the problem is the absorption of categorial differences and other varieties of mentality into the general intellectual system of the religion. In a great religion embracing many races some differences are bound to remain as distinct sects or trends of opinion; but many are absorbed or disappear. One would like to think that those who come from a group with a distinct mentality find this mentality fulfilled in the dominant mentality of their new religion; but one cannot be sure that this is always so. In some cases, however, there would seem to be real acceptance and adaptation. It is noteworthy that there was a real flowering of the Persian mentality within the framework provided by Arab-Islamic culture.

The considerations of the last few paragraphs have a relevance to the contemporary situation. A man faces his particular problems as a member of various communities – religious, political, social, domestic. In some ways the religious is the most important, for it deals with the fundamental aspects of events and is potentially the largest community. As was stated above, a man as he deals with his problems is conditioned by the whole past history of his religious community. He responds to the situation in terms of this history and tradition, not necessarily by a rigorous following of precedents, but rather by an adaptation of the tradition to the new circumstances. Where there is a problem to solve, a solution which has deep roots in the life of the historical organism is to be preferred. This principle has important implications for the conception of missionary work. The Christian missionary movement which began about 1800 did not distinguish between Christian-izing and Europeanizing people. It expected converts not merely to abandon their old religion, but also most of their old culture and mentality. This may have been justified where one was dealing with relatively primitive communities. It is an unsatisfactory and dangerously misleading conception when it is applied to the relations of the great world religions.

Finally we may look at an interesting theoretical point. The revealed scripture (we assume) remains the same from generation to generation, but there is a slight variation in its function, the aspects which are emphasized, and even the interpretation of certain passages. The question may then be raised: Does the verbal form have many potentialities (meanings) in it, which are only gradually realized in the historical organism? Or is it that men read new, presumably corporate, insights into the verbal form? If the latter alternative is nearer the truth, it might be that men attach their insights to the verbal form because of its relationship to the historical organism. It is not an essential part of this study to answer these questions, but they may serve as a transition to the discussion of interpretation in the next chapter.

SIX

THE INTERPRETING OF THE REVELATION

♋

1. Primary Interpretation

The primary and contemporary interpretation of the revelation is inevitably based on the previous intellectual state of the hearers. It has already been argued that a revelation is directed to hearers with a certain outlook, and is in terms of their previous comprehension of the world and human life and of their familiarity with it. The Arabic Qur'an presupposes the many different facets of the Arab mentality. Let us now look at this matter in a different perspective, however, and consider how the Arab mentality led the first Muslims to interpret the text of the Qur'an.

The hearers of any revelation are bound to interpret it in accordance with the vocabulary and grammar of the language which is familiar to them. Sometimes, however, the revelation will need to express ideas that are not familiar to the hearers. In such cases words familiar to the hearers are given a new and extended meaning. One word that has been treated in this way in the Qur'an is *waḥy*, which became a technical term for 'revelation'. Originally, however, it had some more general meaning such as 'making a sign' or 'indicating'. Similarly we know that in pre-Islamic times the normal meaning of the word *kāfir* was 'ungrateful', and it is sometimes used in the Qur'an in this sense. Then it came to have the special meaning of one who was ungrateful to God, and this implied a refusal to acknowledge God as the source of one's life and prosperity. Thus the word becomes the technical term for 'unbeliever', and is frequently used in this way in the Qur'an.

An instructive word in this connection is *tazakkī*, which is usually taken to mean 'almsgiving' or 'purification' or 'purification by almsgiving'. The clue to the solution of the problem is to be found in the remark of an early commentator, Ibn-Zayd, quoted by aṭ-Ṭabarī on 79.18, to the effect that *at-taẓakkī* in the Qur'an means *al-islām*. This is to be understood as saying that *at-taẓakkī* stands for the particular things that were essential to being a Muslim during the Meccan period, such as belief in God, prayer, *ẓakāt* ('alms'), perhaps rising at night. Thus for a time the word indicated exactly what Muhammad's followers were doing. As time went on, however, the religious practice of the community of Muslims became more complex. Some matters, such as rising at night ceased to be obligatory, while new obligations were laid upon them, such as the fast of Ramaḍān. The set of practices designated by *at-taẓakkī* was no longer normal in the community. For the members of the community other terms were used in preference, such as 'believer', 'Muslim', *ḥanīf*. The participle of *taẓakkā* had apparently never been used anyway. The noun and verb also fell out of use, and the precise meaning they had once had was forgotten. The organism in its growth had passed beyond the stage to which this word corresponded, and even the memory of the stage became somewhat hazy.

To the primary interpretation there may also be said to belong an indication of the particular references of verses of the Qur'an. Thus to understand the opening words of sura 80, 'he frowned and turned away, because the blind man came to him', we must know that it was Muhammad who frowned; and it is also useful to know who the blind man was. The Muslims at the time when this was revealed knew both Muhammad and the blind man, and may have already heard about the incident. For those who did not become Muslims until after Muhammad's death, all these things would have to be explained. Similar explanations would be required for the stories of previous messengers. Most members of the community would probably have a slight knowledge of the stories; but gaps and deficiencies in their knowledge would be made good by better-informed members. In time men would specialize in the collecting of information of this kind, and might even seek it beyond the community from Jews and Christians. All this interpretation and elaboration, however, may be said to be an activity of the community as a whole.

Many verses of the Qur'an refer to common experiences of

the Muslim community, such as the opposition of the pagan
Meccans before the Hijra and of the Jews at Medina, and the
fighting at Badr and Uḥud. To those who were Muslims when
the revelations came, the application must have been obvious.
Those who only became Muslims much later, however,
required to know a little about the historical circumstances.
Gradually the more intelligent would have in their minds a
rough historical framework into which to fit events and
incidents, though, where the Arab episodic conception of
history dominated, this framework would be of the simplest.
While the commentators preserve some information about the
'occasion' on which particular passages were revealed, much
less information of this kind has been preserved than one would
have hoped for; and there are contradictions in what has been
preserved. It is also possible that some of the 'occasions' are
no more than the conjectures of later Muslim scholars.

Where the revelation consisted of direct commands, the
response would follow immediately on the primary interpretation, that is, on understanding the words. An instance
would be the command (in sura 74) to rise at night for devo-
tional exercises. Even here, however, the precise way in which
a Muslim carried out a command would be influenced by what
he saw Muhammad and the other Muslims doing. At some
points the stories in the Qur'an may be said to contain indirect
commands – for example, when a character in a story is presented as worthy of imitation. A case of this would be the
attitude of Jacob under misfortune, which is summarized in his
phrase 'Fitting patience!' [12.18, 83]. For such an indirect
command to be applicable to someone he must in part have
identified himself with the character in the story. He must see,
that is to say, that in his personal misfortune it is appropriate
that he should behave as Jacob behaved. Here again, of course,
the practical response will depend to some extent on the attitude
and practice of the community as a whole – though less so than
in the case of direct commands.

There is a sense, then, in which the function of the revelation
is not complete until there has been at least this primary interpretation. God, we believe, intends the revelation to be effective where men make a positive response to it; but before they
can make a positive response they must have understood the

revelation and seen its relevance to their own lives. Thus interpretation is necessarily involved in the response, and is also an integral activity of the historical organism of revelation.[1]

2. Adaptive and Systematizing Interpretation

The previous section should have made it clear that the interpretation of the revelation is intimately bound up with the ongoing life of the community; that is, in particular, that the interpretation of the Qur'an is an integral part of the historical organism of Islam. In the decades and centuries after the death of Muhammad there was a vast expansion of the community of Muslims. It came to number millions from many races spread over a large area of the earth's surface. As the community expanded, its life became one of ever-increasing complexity. The basic responses or basic patterns of living were already settled, but they could be elaborated and applied in different ways. This may be called an adaptive interpretation of the revelation, and such interpretations become necessary as the development of the community brings new situations and new problems. Although the interpretation is new, however, in the sense that it has not previously been expressed thus, it has all along been implicit in the revelation – at least according to the dominant view.

In the first century or two of Islam the practical and legal adaptation of the revelation received most attention. The work of governing and administering justice had to be carried on, and there was a body of keen Muslims who insisted that this work should be based on Qur'anic principles. The adaptation consisted in the application of the general principles found in the Qur'an to particular new situations and circumstances; the principles had, of course, from the first been applied to various particular matters. In this process of adaptation it was found that the Qur'an had to be supplemented by the *sunna* or standard practice of Muhammad, for which evidence was obtained from the Traditions. The Traditions then came to be regarded as a kind of secondary revelation. The underlying assumption was presumably that Muhammad's practice would be in accordance with his understanding of the revelation, and that, since he was the recipient of the revelation and so closest to it, his understanding of it would be better than that of other

72

Muslims. In this way the Islamic community elaborated a legal system for itself on the basis of the revelation.

An interesting new interpretation is the doctrine of the uncreatedness of the Qur'an. Muslims had always held that the Qur'an was the word or speech of God, for this was implied by some of the verbal forms of the text. For a century it probably did not occur to anyone to ask whether the Qur'an was created or uncreated; at least there is no record of such a question in the early days. The first person to allege that the Qur'an was created is said to have been put to death about a hundred years after Muhammad's death. The discussion of the question became fiercer in the early 'Abbāsid period, doubtless because of all the adaptive interpretation of the revelation that had been taking place. This work of interpretation and adaptation itself produced a new situation and a new problem. There was a practical problem which might be indicated by the question: Should the adaptation of Islamic principles to a new situation be the work of the imam or leader of the community in the light of his (some would say, divinely inspired) insight into the needs of the situation, or should it be the work of those who had made a deep study of the Qur'an and the practice of Muhammad? In view of their respective tasks it was not surprising that the 'secretaries' or civil servants who carried out the orders of the caliph should have favoured the first alternative, while the main body of scholars or ulema should have favoured the second.

This practical problem with its political ramifications forced the community of Muslims to answer the question whether the Qur'an, the word of God, was created or uncreated. To say the Qur'an was created meant that it was not an essential expression of God's nature, since he might presumably have created it otherwise; and a corollary would be that a divinely-inspired leader might properly at times override the principles stated in the Qur'an. On the other hand, if the Qur'an is the uncreated word of God, it expresses his essential nature, and no one who is divinely-inspired can go against it. This latter view probably also entails that principles to deal with any conceivable situation are implicit in the Qur'an. The two views are, of course, the basis of the division of the Islamic community into Shī'ites and Sunnites; and there is truth in both. Up till now the Sunnites appear on the whole to have been more effective in practice, but they have developed a rigidity from which it would seem only an inspired leader can deliver them. The Shī'ites were right in emphasizing the need for an inspired leader, whether in the political or the intellectual field. Where the imam is also an absolute ruler, there is a danger that he may lead the community away from its roots in the revelation; but most actual Shī'ite communities guard against this.

Besides the practical needs which were met by further interpretation of the revelation, the community of Muslims had also intellectual needs. The fundamental need is for an intellectual world-view that is in accordance both with the revelation and with one's general intellectual outlook. Intellectual difficulties were probably felt most keenly by those who became Muslims after having belonged to other religious traditions, since they came from an intellectual background somewhat different from that of the Arabs to whom the Qur'an was first addressed. These intellectual difficulties led to the development of theology; but in early Islam, theology was usually also linked with practical questions.

At both the practical and intellectual levels men look for a measure of consistency. From this requirement stems the work of systematization, which may also be regarded as a form of interpretation, since to systematize often means the selection of those interpretations of the revelation that are capable of being harmonized with one another. The simplest form of systematization is the composition of creeds. In Christianity creeds have mostly had an official position through the decisions of church councils. In Islam, on the other hand, the authority of a creed was simply that of the theologian who had formulated it. If he was a leading figure, however, in one of the great schools, the school would normally accept his creed, and thereafter it would have the authority of the school. In the formulation of a creed the theologian has to decide such questions as whether the doctrine of the createdness or the uncreatedness of the Qur'an harmonizes better with the other beliefs of Muslims. Before such a doctrine is included in a creed there has usually been much discussion. The discussion will have ranged over a wide field. The verses of the Qur'an supporting one or other view will have been considered; and matters of grammar and lexicography will have been adduced to justify one interpretation rather than another. If one traces the arguments on a single topic over the period of a century or two, one finds that the formulation of a doctrine only takes place within a vast context of intellectual effort.

The consistency of the theological system is linked with the unity of the community. It happens that different groups want to make different adaptations to new circumstances, usually because they have different economic interests or a different intellectual background or a combination of the two. This may lead to a serious dispute within the community, especially if one or both feels that something vital is threatened by the other. A genuine resolution of the difficulty should allow each side to retain what it feels to be essential. Where this is not attained and one or other continues to feel the threat, there grows up a will to disunity, and a division within the community becomes inevitable. This happened in Islam between the Khārijites and the Shī'ites, for example, and again between the Shī'ites and the Sunnites. Thus failure to discover a credal formulation which is harmonious, and which contains the elements which each side regards as essential, leads to a split in the community.

There is also, however, in every vigorous community a strong will to unity. This is often, perhaps always, linked with a belief, which need not be altogether explicit, that the community is a charismatic one.[2] This may also be described as a belief that it is only through the community that the individual's life becomes meaningful. For men with such a belief it is important to keep within the community as many people as possible of those who share the same basic patterns of response, while tolerating various shades of opinion beyond the basic patterns. For this reason doctrine becomes complex; it has to be acceptable to different groups by containing all that each holds to be vital. In this matter it is interesting to note a difference between the community of Islam and that of Eastern Christianity or Orthodoxy. In the latter case, as is emphasized by the name of 'Orthodox', there is a rigid unity based on the acceptance of a complex creed. Islam, on the other hand, is less rigid and less unified, in that there are several legal rites; but it has shown great ability to maintain its unity over centuries.

3. Methods of Interpretation

When the Qur'an was first revealed it was normally interpreted by the Muslims according to the obvious and literal meaning of the words. When sectional differences appeared, however, each party tried to find verses to support its case, and then interpreted the verses in such a way as to make the support more convincing. All sorts of arguments were used in these partisan interpretations to begin with, and all the various groups had in common was their acceptance of the Qur'an as the touchstone to which disagreements were to be referred. A point could always be scored by showing that an opponent had been inconsistent with himself. Apart from this, however, there was little agreement as to what types of argument were admissible and what types were not.

Even when a set of sectional interpretations has a high degree of consistency, it may yet be based on principles or forms of argument which are not acceptable to other sections of the community. The future of such a section then comes to depend on whether it decides to organize itself independently of the other sections of the community, or whether it still feels that it belongs to the community and wants to achieve harmony with the other sections. Some extreme Khārijite sects, like the Azāriqa, considered that all other Muslims had adopted views which were incompatible with Islam and had thus put themselves outside the community of Muslims; and so only they, the Azāriqa, were now Muslims. In a case like this there could be no question of attempting to harmonize the sectarian interpretations with those of the rest of the community. After a time some groups of Khārijites abandoned the more uncompromising aspects of Khārijite doctrine, and the community as a whole then accepted the Khārijite insistence on the importance of upright conduct.[3] On the other hand, where a group feels that it and other groups, however misguided these seem to be, belong together, then the possibility of a set of harmonizing interpretations is still open. To achieve this, however, usually requires some degree of sophistication. Apart from the superficial points at issue, groups may differ in their categorial presuppositions, and these affect their whole method of arguing and interpreting. Thus harmony can only be attained where the

76

groups are aware not merely of the objects of their thought, but also of their intellectual methods of dealing with these objects.

A growing awareness of this kind can be traced in the history of Qur'anic exegesis (*tafsīr*). There were many discussions about the normal and metaphorical usages of language, and about the literal (or obvious – *ẓāhir*) and esoteric (*bāṭin*) senses of words and passages. Some of these points will be considered in the next chapter. For the moment it will be more useful to look at the contrast between the general character of early Islamic exegesis and certain methods of interpretation that are favoured at the present time.

Much early Islamic exegesis may be described as 'atomistic'. A verse or even a phrase may be treated as a self-subsistent atom, taken in isolation from its context, and used to prove some legal or theological point. There may be some connection between this exegetical atomism and the cosmological atomism noted above (p. 32 f.). Both might derive from a categorial assumption that a thing is what it is independently of its relations to other things. This leads to profound philosophical questions which are outside the scope of the present study. The point of immediate concern is the application of this atomistic conception to the theory of truth. The theory implied by the practice of the early Islamic scholars would seem to be that truth and falsehood belong to statements in isolation from all other statements, and can be known by considering the isolated statement. This theory is modified slightly by allowing that pre-Islamic usage of Arabic must be taken into consideration; that is, an unusual meaning cannot be given to a word in a verse of the Qur'an unless this meaning is supported by a line of pre-Islamic poetry. Apart from this, however, one derives the meaning of a verse from the verse itself and not from looking at its relation to other verses, either contextually or in respect of similarities.

An atomistic exegesis of the kind described usually tolerates inconsistencies. This is not true, however, of all early Muslim scholars. Those who allowed some use of reason – for instance, in drawing inferences from Qur'anic statements – usually assumed that, if there was a contradiction between two interpretations or their implications, then one of the interpretations must be wrong. On the other hand, most of the conservative

Muslim scholars hesitated to draw inferences and accepted both of two statements, where other scholars might feel that the implications of the two statements showed them to be inconsistent. In this way there appears to be a connection between the atomistic tendency and the acceptance of inconsistency which was noted above as a feature of the Arab mentality (p. 34 f.). The connection may arise from the fact that the acceptance of inconsistency is in line with a concrete, poetic way of thinking which is in sharp contrast to abstract, logical thinking. Since the latter deals with things in classes, and looks for common features, qualities and relationships it opposes the atomistic tendency, whereas concrete or poetic thinking deals with individuals as individuals, that is, in relative isolation. The acceptance of inconsistency as necessary to convey the richness of the real world is not restricted to Arabs, but appears to be part of a general Semitic outlook, being also found in the Old Testament.

To be distinguished from atomistic interpretation of the Qur'an is what may be called contextual interpretation. This consists in studying and interpreting the verse in its context within the sura or section of a sura, and also within its historical context, that is, in relation to the events which were the 'occasion' of the revelation of this particular passage. Apart from the cases where there is some traditional information about the occasion of revelation, modern scholars consider it possible to learn something about the occasion of many passages, where there is no traditional material, by making inferences from the words of the passage and our general knowledge of the course of events. Thus contextual interpretation with its historical emphasis is congenial to the modern scholar, but several of the Muslim exegetes practised this form of interpretation, and argued that a certain meaning of a particular verse must be adopted because of the meaning of other verses in the same passage.[4]

From contextual interpretation one might further distinguish 'global interpretation'. In some respects this is a form of contextual interpretation, but its special feature is that it insists that what we are interpreting is not a particular verse but the Qur'anic vision of reality as a whole. This means that the context has become the whole of the Qur'an and the whole historical organism of Islam. A global interpretation in this sense would seem to imply that the interpretations of later generations have been potentially present in the revelation from the first. For this reason no special emphasis is placed on the 'original' meaning of any verse.

The points just made lead on to further questions about the possibility and justification of 'non-historical' interpretations. The most obvious case of this is the interpretation of many Old Testament passages as referring to Jesus, especially as some of them – like those about 'the suffering servant' – may originally have been taken to refer to the whole people of Israel personified. The justification of such interpretations is that there is in the course of history a repetition of patterns. In many cases, however, this is not a mere repetition but a recapitulation of the past in order to base a further stage of development on it.[5] These facts are familiar to us at a lower level. The human child in its early development repeats most of the evolutional development of life from lower forms. Again, in the education of a man, he has to 'repeat' or assimilate all that the human race has learnt in the past about a topic before he can go on to do fruitful research in that topic. In so far, then, as one looks at the world globally, the later patterns may be 'repetitions' of earlier patterns, even though they may have developed beyond anything which those familiar with the earlier patterns would recognize. These matters will be discussed further in the next chapter in connection with the significance of the figure of Abraham in Islam.

SEVEN

REVELATION AS 'DIAGRAMMATIC'

☽

1. Islamic Dimensions of the Problem of Religious Language

It was impossible for Muslim scholars to avoid for long the questions raised for thinking men by religious language. The questions are also raised by other human attempts to speak about what is not sensuously perceived, but they are more serious in the religious field, since some of the main religious assertions concern non-sensuous realities. Human language, however, begins with the objects of sensuous perception, and when it is applied to non-sensuous realities, there has to be some explicit or implicit comparison of these with sensuous phenomena. This is a common feature of all poetry, and pre-Islamic Arab poetry was no stranger to it. The poet regularly compares his horse or his camel to a wild animal, to a cloud, or to some other object familiar to desert-dwellers. He may compare a tedious night to an animal slowly raising itself up. Such a figure of speech as the last helps us to realize how the night felt to those who experienced it. There is no danger of confusion, for we know what a night is, and that it is not in fact an animal.

It is more difficult, however, when the matter spoken about is a reality of which man has no sensuous awareness in the usual sense (that is, apart from inferences from sensuous experience). How is one to understand such a phrase as 'the hand of God'? How indeed is one to understand the word 'God' (or '*the* deity') in a world where there are sensuously-perceived deities (idols) in material temples? For a time it seems to be possible to retain a naive outlook .One uses the words adequately, that is, not expecting to see a fleshly hand and the like; and one does not raise the awkward questions about the relation of words to the realities signified. In other terms, one is unaware of the distinction between the literal and metaphorical usages of words, but in practice no confusion arises from this absence of awareness.

The troubles begin when some men become aware of this distinction and ask questions. To those with this more sophisticated outlook a man who clings to the naive view becomes an 'anthropomorphist' or a 'corporealist' (*mushabbih, mujassim*), because he makes God resemble man and declares him to have a body. The naive man, on the other hand, probably feels that to deny God is like man and has a body is tantamount to denying that he is a real being. There is some justification for the naive view, since it is difficult to give an account of metaphor without admitting a degree of unreality in the object metaphorically described. A long night may be like a heavy ungainly beast; and the metaphor adds to our knowledge, since we have a general idea, apart from the metaphor, of what a night is. In the case of God, on the other hand, if we say he does not really have a hand and is not really a body, is there anything left? One of the early attempts by Muslim scholars to deal with this difficulty was to say that the anthropomorphic terms in the Qur'an were to be understood *bi-lā kayf*, 'without how', that is, without specifying the manner (literal or metaphorical) in which the word or phrase is to be understood. This might be regarded as an attempt to maintain the naive view, but in a sophisticated way.

The opponents of the naive view, who called the upholders of the latter 'anthropomorphists' and 'corporealists', apparently wanted to assert the spiritual and immaterial nature of God. They may also have wanted to assert his transcendence of the time-process. Anthropomorphism, or making God resemble man (*tashbīh*), offended against their general conception of God as all-powerful, all-knowing and ever-living; they presumably thought of men as limited in power and knowledge and in the duration of life. The anthropomorphic view also created insuperable obstacles for their rational proofs of the existence of God. To the more sophisticated scholars, then, with their rational ways of thinking, the naive view seemed to be a denial of the existence of God. To the naive, on the other hand, the sophisticated appeared to be denying the simple basic truths which had come to them by revelation. Since each side felt that a central belief was threatened by the other side, the dispute was a bitter one.

On the whole Muslim thinkers have placed the chief emphasis on God's transcendence, especially in the sense of his absolute difference from man (*mukhālafa*). A few have exaggerated transcendence to such an extent that it becomes difficult for them to show how there can be a real contact between God and the world. The main body of Islam, of course, has always insisted on God's constant activity in the world in the sense of his control and indeed determination of all events. Thus most Muslims have managed to hold the balance between pure transcendence and pure immanence. All have accepted the formulations of the revealed scripture. Some deal with the anthropomorphic terms of the Qur'an by permitting metaphorical interpretation in some carefully defined cases. Others adopt a form of the principle of 'not specifying how', and, while accepting the terms which actually occur in the scriptures, refuse to allow analogous terms which might be inferred from them and refuse to discuss the manner in which the terms are employed.

At the other end of the spectrum there have been sufis who, like mystics in other religions, spoke much of the immanence of the divine in the human. A phrase that was much discussed was *takhalluq bi-akhlāq Allāh*, which might be rendered 'characterization by the characters (or good qualities) of God'. The theologian al-Ghazālī has written an interesting essay, *Al-maqṣad al-asnā*, in which he endeavours to show that, without implying any resemblance between man and God, man may yet be 'characterized by the characters of God'. Here a great thinker struggles with an obstinate problem. The whole theological tradition to which he belonged insisted that man and God are absolutely different, and yet his heart convinced him that the highest human values must somehow be present in divinity.

These brief indications show how deeply Muslim scholars were concerned with the problems raised by religious language, and also show the particular form taken by the problems in an Islamic context.

2. The 'Diagrammatic' use of Language

The problems connected with the use of religious language continue to concern men, and look like being even more discussed during the next half century. The controversies among Christian theologians about 'demythologizing' may be said to deal with the 'translation' of Christian belief from the thought-forms of the New Testament period to the thought-forms of contemporary Europe and America. This presupposes the existence of a reality beyond the language, indeed of a reality which is only partially communicated by the language. Similar problems are likely to face Islam in the near future as more Muslims are given an education in occidental science and technology.

The present study is not the place for a full discussion of this matter, and I shall therefore briefly make some of the points I have already made more fully in *Truth in the Religions* (especially pp. 124-30). The heart of the problem appears to be the nature of metaphor. When metaphor is used in poetry, we know, for example, that the night is not really a huge beast. Metaphor is also used by scientists in various ways. By the name of 'heuristic model' it may suggest fresh lines of experiment, some of which may prove fruitful. It may also be used to expound recondite mysteries to the non-scientist, as when it is said that light is in some ways like waves and in other ways like particles. In the latter example light for the scientist is really neither waves nor particles but really is a 'something' which obeys certain equations (of which some may resemble those for waves and others those for particles). Because of such facts the man of today, familiar with the scientific outlook, tends to feel that, when a thing is only described by metaphors, it is unreal. In particular many men of today consider that the word 'God' does not stand for anything real. This association of the metaphorical with the unreal is, of course, by no means the only factor leading to rejection of belief in God, but it is one of the factors.

Even the religious believer, however, has to admit that there is an element of unreality in the application of anthropomorphic language to God. God does not really have a hand with flesh and bones and muscles. The ordinary Muslim, when he hears the Qur'an recited, in some sense hears the speech of God; but he does not directly hear God speaking by means of sound waves in the atmosphere. Thus even the believer accepts a degree of unreality in religious language. He differs, however, from the person who identifies metaphor with unreality in that he claims that religious language does give man some positive knowledge of non-sensuous reality. It would therefore be desirable to find some more adequate way to express this relation of language to reality in which, beyond the unreality, some positive truth was conveyed. I want to suggest that the conception of a diagram meets this desideratum.

In a diagram certain shapes and colours are used to convey certain truths. In a genealogical table a certain arrangement of lines shows the precise relationship of members of a family to one another. In many countries railways are indicated by straight lines, with circles or crosses for stations. The London Underground has often used a diagram with a number of parallel lines, and another set of parallel lines crossing them, together with various connecting lines. These represent the underground system with its different 'lines' or routes, each 'line' having a different colour. The stations are marked, and the traveller is shown where it is possible to change from one 'line' to another. Much information is given with absolute accuracy – the order of the stations on each 'line', the interchange points, the possible routes from one station to another. Yet there is also much unreality. The bends on the tracks are not shown, the distances of the stations from one another are not accurately shown, the actual tracks are not the colour shown, and so on. Despite this unreality, however, which the average traveller has learnt to allow for anyway, the diagram conveys with full accuracy all the information it was designed to convey.

Much the same is true of maps. Rivers, coastlines and the like are represented by outlines that are similar but on a much smaller scale. The shape of the island of Cyprus on a map is the shape one sees from the air. When a map is of a relatively large part of the earth's surface, however, the complications due to the spheroidal shape of the earth are more serious, and the map-maker has to select which geographical features he will represent with greatest accuracy. Apart from those features which are represented by similar shapes on a smaller scale, there are many which are indicated by purely conventional signs or colours. In general, however, maps like diagrams are designed to convey information, but only within certain limits. A good map or diagram completely fulfils this limited purpose to the planned degree of accuracy. There may be much in it of which we can say 'Things are not really like that'; but the positive information it is intended to convey, it conveys truthfully.

Religious language – both assertions and the ideas or terms used in these assertions – resembles the diagram or map in various ways, and in this sense may be called 'diagrammatic'. The resemblance is both in respect of the element of unreality and also of the positive conveying of information. On the positive side, to put it briefly, religious language gives man sufficient information about the nature of the universe to enable him to conduct his life in it satisfactorily. On the other hand it does not give him anything like all the answers needed by his intellectual curiosity. Religious language can only be properly appreciated by those who admit the limitations of the human intellect. Once this admission has been made, however, it can be seen that religious language (in the best examples) is fully adequate for its restricted practical purpose.

It may be objected that, while the diagram or map follows conventions, natural or artificial, consciously adopted by the person making it, there are no such consciously adopted conventions in the case of religious language. Now, in so far as the religious language of revealed scriptures is held to have come from a supernatural source – the view in different forms of Jews, Christians and Muslims – it may be said that this supernatural source designed the language for the limited practical purpose in view. Such an answer to the objection, however, only pushes the problem back a stage. We human beings are attempting to describe non-sensuous or supersensuous reality in anthropomorphic terms; and the point of this discussion of the diagrammatic use of language is to insist that the revealed scriptures are sufficient for practical guidance in the business of living, but do not give us complete intellectual satisfaction. Even the terms 'God' and 'revelation' are diagrammatic. To use anthropomorphic terms of God and say he has a 'will' and 'power' is helpful to man for the conduct of his life, since it gives him a confidence in the course of events. To speak of God 'revealing' truths to man reduces man's anxiety since he feels he is being guided by something greater than himself, something which can be trusted. Beyond this, however, man's intellect receives little satisfaction.

3. The Significance of Abraham in the Qur'an

The considerations which have just been advanced will help us towards a more adequate appreciation of the significance of the figure of Abraham in the Qur'an. This is the more necessary, since the scientific historian of today is inclined to dismiss much of what the Qur'an says about Abraham as purely imaginary, and therefore valueless. He may say, for example, that the conception of the religion of Abraham was 'invented' to justify Muhammad's break with the Jews shortly before the battle of Badr in 624, and to meet the Jewish criticisms of the Qur'an. The various Qur'anic assertions about Abraham are, of course, primarily assertions about this-worldly events. Nevertheless they are 'diagrammatic' in that they give man guidance about the ordering of his life in relation to the supersensuous, while they do not give him much intellectual satisfaction. What follows here is far from being a complete discussion of the significance of the Qur'anic figure of Abraham, but merely indicates some of the more important positive aspects.

The Qur'anic claim that Islam is identical with the pure religion of Abraham is worthy of serious consideration [e.g. 2.133/29]. The religions of Judaism, Christianity and Islam may all be said to have their beginning in the religious experience of Abraham. Such a statement has an implication which is strange and surprising to most Jews and Christians, namely, that these religions have their origin in an experience which is temporally prior to anything which can be called Judaism. As the Qur'an puts it: 'Abraham was neither a Jew nor a Christian, but a *hanīf*, a *muslim*, not one of the idolaters' [3.67/0]. Europeans tend to think of Old Testament religion (apart from idolatry) as one religion, and are familiar with the phrase 'the God of Abraham, of Isaac and of Jacob', so that it is a shock to be told that Abraham was not a Jew. Yet (as noted briefly on p. 51) this is the case. Some would say that Judaism began after the exile; some would allow that it began with the Law revealed to Moses; a few might agree to identify it with the religion of the children of Israel. Yet even on the last interpretation Abraham was not a Jew, since Israel or Jacob was his grandson.

It is, of course, obvious that Abraham was not a Christian in any normal sense. If it is argued that there is a continuity of development throughout the Old Testament, this is precisely the point that the present argument is trying to make; but it follows that the earliest experience is pre-Judaic, pre-Mosaic and pre-Israelite.

At the strictly historical level the evidence is of the slightest. It has been suggested that there was no single individual called Abraham, such as he has been described, and that the name rather represents a tribe or body of people. Even if this is so – which is far from certain – it is a secondary matter. The important thing is that there was a human experience in which a man or a body of men responded to an 'inner voice' or 'revelation', which they believed to come from a beneficent being superior to themselves on whom they were dependent. This pattern of response to the divine prompting was singled out by Paul as an essential basis of Christianity; he insisted, referring to the book of *Genesis*, 15.6, that 'Abraham believed God, and it was accounted unto him for righteousness' [*Romans*, 4.3; cf. *Galatians*, 3.6], and that Christians must follow Abraham in this respect. From the initial response of Abraham to something of the nature of revelation there has sprung what we may call the historical organism of the religion of Abraham, which includes within itself the separate historical organisms of the three religions. In the Qur'an the word *ḥanīf* indicates an adherent of this basic monotheism, while *muslim* in a non-technical sense is precisely 'one surrendered (to God)' and therefore almost synonymous. There can be no Jewish or Christian objection to these terms once it is admitted that 'the historical organism of the religion of Abraham' is a valid and important concept.

The Qur'anic conception of the religion of Abraham, however, has a negative corollary, and this – many occidentals will feel – must give us pause. The corollary is that among the Christians and Jews contemporary with Muhammad the pure religion of Abraham had been corrupted. The actual statements of the Qur'an about the corruption of the scriptures and similar matters do not go nearly so far as the later elaborations of the doctrine of corruption. It is, of course, obvious to occidental scholars that there has been no corruption of the text of the

Bible such as has been maintained by some Muslims. Yet it is also possible to understand the Qur'anic phrases 'diagrammatically' and as instances of something more fundamental. Even if it is allowed that each 'revelation' as it came to each member of the great series of prophets was pure and undistorted, yet in the course of a generation or two distortions might easily creep in. It was natural, for example, that Christians should be concerned with the intellectual defence of their faith against Jews; but some of the Christians involved had a feeling of inferiority, and to compensate for this the Christian case was exaggerated in subtle ways. Every religious movement, however pure to begin with, is liable to distortion in the course of a generation or two. Evidence of this is the Jewish denial of Jesus, the Christian refusal to acknowledge Muhammad as a prophet, and the Muslim erection of defences against Judaism and Christianity. Had the Jews and Christians of the time retained their religion in its pure form, they would have recognized the working of God in and through Muhammad, as Waraqa is said to have done. To this extent the Qur'anic conception of 'corruption' is justified.

Another important feature of the Qur'anic picture of Abraham is his rejection of the idolatry of his father and his father's people. This is mentioned several times in the Qur'an [e.g. 37.83/1-101/99], though it does not occur in the Biblical picture. Now idol-worship or 'the old religion' is essentially a worship of the powers of nature, especially the fertility seen in male and female sexuality. In such worship there is much that is good, since it includes an acknowledgement of man's dependence on powers greater than himself. Yet it was made clear to the religious leaders of the Israelites in the Old Testament that there could be no gradual development from this old religion to pure monotheism, but that at some point there had to be a break. The Old Testament prophets, therefore, vigorously denounce the worship of idols. Yet much that was valuable in the old religion was tacitly incorporated into the new monotheism, not least the conception of sacrifice; and sacrifice came to have a central place in the New Testament. This general truth about human nature – that at certain junctures a break is necessary, if there is to be progress – is 'diagrammatically' expressed by the Qur'an in the accounts of Abra-

88

ham's rejection of idols. It was likewise a feature of Muhammad's career. For long he hoped that there would be a smooth transition from the old religion to the new monotheism; but after the affair of 'the satanic verses' he realized that it was impossible.

Another un-Biblical feature of the Qur'anic account of Abraham is his connection with Mecca and his foundation of the Ka'ba there [2.124/18-129/3]. Again, though this does not provide material for scientific history of the Abrahamic period, it conveys important truths 'diagrammatically'. Above all, it is asserting that the religious impulse which originated or restored the worship at the Ka'ba in the distant past is identical with the response of Abraham to 'revelation' and with the revived response of this type being made by the Muslims. This means, it would seem, that while there was corruption and distortion in pre-Islamic religion at Mecca, some elements of truth might have survived. The retention in Islam of old rites like the circumambulation of the Ka'ba and many pilgrimage ceremonies may be regarded as a practical application of the theoretical principle.

Despite the connection of Abraham with Mecca, the Qur'an does not specifically state that any Arabs were descended from him. Later Muslim scholars, however, linked up traditional Arab genealogies with those in the Old Testament, and took the view that the Northern Arabs were descended from Ishmael. It certainly is true that most of the Arabs are racially connected with other Semitic peoples, and have inherited much of the same mentality, culture and religion.

As one looks to the future one sees the urgency of fuller mutual understanding between the three great religions here considered. In the achievement of such understanding it would seem that the conception of 'the religion of Abraham' has an important part to play. For one thing this conception places the three religions on an equal footing, and avoids the appearance of making Islam the poor relation of Judaism and Christianity. It also indicates how the essential experience or 'pure religion' of Abraham – a positive response to divine promptings – is the basic element shared by Jews, Christians and Muslims. The conception further makes it possible for us to speak of the historical organism of the religion of Abraham, and to see that this is to be regarded as a single organism whose three chief 'organs' have become partly separate from one another. Finally let it be emphasized that there is nothing fanciful about this use of the figure of Abraham, but that it is 'diagrammatically' expressing very profound aspects of ultimate reality.

EIGHT

THE INFLUENCE OF THE REVELATION

ॐ

1. The Qur'an and the Islamic Way of Life

To understand the influence of the Qur'anic revelation it is necessary to look more fully at the historical aspects of 'the historical organism of Islam'. It is common to speak of the expansion of Islam as if this went hand in hand with the expansion of the Islamic state; but this was not so. There was indeed a rapid expansion of the caliphal state, so that a century after Muhammad's death it stretched from the south of France through Spain and North Africa to north-west India and Transoxiana or Central Asia. This expansion, however, was essentially military and political, not religious. To begin with only the conquering and occupying armies were Muslim – even restricted to Muslim Arabs at first; but the demands on manpower drove the leaders to accept as soldiers many converts to Islam, chiefly from the Berbers in the west and from the Persians in the east. The occupation was followed slowly and gradually by conversions from among the civilian population. Thus throughout the Empire there was a growing body of people deeply committed to living according to the basic patterns of the original response to the Qur'an. To employ the terms suggested above (p. 9), one might say that response to the revelation was gradually spreading in the ectosoma, and the ectosoma gradually being incorporated in the endosoma.

The complexity of the issues being discussed here is well illustrated by a fact connected with the military expansion. It is not unusual for religion to support military activity by giving soldiers courage in the face of death; and Islam certainly did this. The Muslims regarded themselves as 'fighting in the way of God' or, as Europeans like to express it, in a 'holy war'; and it was further believed that those who fell thus fighting were martyrs and would certainly go to Paradise. Beyond this, however, the conception of the holy war gave direction to the whole course of military operations. The aim of the holy war was not simply to defeat the enemy, but, once that had been done, to bring him to accept Islam if he was an Arab pagan, and to bring him to accept the status of 'protected person' (*dhimmī*) if he was a non-Arab and a member of a scriptural religion. Those who became Muslims or *dhimmīs* could no longer be attacked by Muslims; and therefore the warlike energies of the Arabs, which had been developed through life in the desert, and which could not simply be suppressed, had to be directed continually outwards. This gave impetus to the expansion.

The influence of Islam is best seen in its permeation and domination of the culture of the Middle East. L. S. Thornton has written:[1]

> 'religion enters into the texture of its human environment
> in such a way that a single pattern of life is woven out
> of the various elements through a unifying power which
> characterizes the religion in question.'

This was presumably written with Judaism and Christianity chiefly in mind and without any special thought about Islam; yet it is appropriate to Islam. Many elements of culture already present in the lands occupied by the Muslims were brought into Islam. This might be done by converts who had previously been versed in some aspect of the former culture; or Muslim scholars might learn from their contacts with those who adhered to their previous faith. Both these methods contributed to the bringing of much Greek intellectual culture into Islam. Whatever route was followed, however, such aspects of alien cultures as were accepted into Islam were fitted into the pattern of life of the Muslim community, and into the intellectual worldview based on the Qur'an. In course of time it was realized that the whole life of the community depended on maintaining the centrality of the Qur'an. This was made explicit when, a year or two before 850, the caliph, al-Mutawakkil, abandoned the policy of the Inquisition (Miḥna) by which leading officials were required to make public profession of their belief in the createdness of the Qur'an.

The unifying and integrating power of Islam is remarkably illustrated by its assimilation of alien cultural elements. The military and political expansion of the Arabs produced a new cultural situation in which many diverse cultures and sub-cultures found themselves jostling with one another within the framework provided by the Islamic Empire. Perhaps the most important aspect of this framework was the vastness of the area within which communications were easy. This led to a great intermingling of peoples and their cultures. Thus a new cultural situation came about, as it were naturally, following on the military and political expansion; and Islam responded to the challenge of this new situation by accepting most of the extraneous elements and integrating them into its own organism. Persons from many different environments were welcomed as Muslims, and brought with them various cultural elements. In nearly every case whatever was compatible with Islam was added to the common stock; and the end result was a high degree of cultural homogeneity throughout the Islamic heart-lands.

Though the main expansion of Islam, politically speaking, was during the century after Muhammad's death, there was further gradual expansion in later centuries, especially to East and West Africa and to South-East Asia (Malaysia and Indonesia). Many peoples in these regions have become part of the historical organism of Islam, even of the endosoma. In these peripheral regions, however, there are many local variations of Islam; and, though these variations are not usually questioned in the region itself, they have seldom been officially accepted in the heartlands. Thus the heartlands have not yet taken full cognizance of the periphery. The process of integration continues, however, and with improved communications the Islam of the periphery is likely to become more homogeneous with the Islam of the heartlands.

According to pre-Islamic Arab ideas this gradual development of Islam and its assimilation of alien cultures might seem to be a decline, in that it is a departure from its pristine purity. The opposite is rather the case, however, and the development is the actualization of what was potentially present from the first. This point may be reinforced by another quotation from L. S. Thornton:[2]

93

'Cultures, however, are in one degree or another transitory. For, unlike the major uniformities of nature, they are human adaptations of nature which are liable to lose their relevance and their suitability under the changing conditions of historical development. For this reason a living religion shows its vitality by assimilating itself to successive cultures through the advance of the centuries, whereas a religion which has less vitality may become fossilized in a particular form of culture, reinforcing it where it should have broken through to new forms of expression.'

What is here called 'fossilization' is easily illustrated in most religions. It is not certain, however, that 'vitality' is something fixed in terms of more and less. It seems rather that at certain points which are usually unpredictable a partly fossilized religion responds positively to a new challenge and experiences 'revival' and revitalization.

2. The Failure of Christianity in the Middle East

An important part of the achievement of Islam in the Middle East has been its displacement of Christianity as the focus of cultural life. Large regions where the populations mostly belonged to the endosoma of Christianity now have populations which belong even more entirely to the endosoma of Islam. It is necessary to look at the reasons for this carefully. Sufficient has already been said in this study about the strength of Islam. If we are to follow Arnold Toynbee, however, the major reason will be the internal weakness of Christianity.

The root of the Christian failure is to be looked for in the treatment of the 'oriental' Christians. The term 'oriental' will here be restricted to those Christians whose native language was other than Greek, and in particular, Syriac, Coptic or Armenian. These languages were spoken by sufficient people for them to become literary languages and thereby the centre of a culture or sub-culture. In this they differed from some of the languages of Asia Minor which continued to be spoken, but which were replaced by Greek for literary purposes. Many of the 'orientals', especially the theologians among them, also used Greek for serious writing; but their thinking was essenti-

94

ally in the categories and concepts proper to the mentality associated with each language. Differences of mentality led to differences of theological formulation on various matters; and when these came before ecumenical councils, the 'orientals' were usually outvoted by the 'Greeks'. In the course of time the 'orientals' found themselves declared heretics and sometimes even outlawed from the Byzantine Empire.

The most important groups of 'heretics' were those often known as Monophysites and Nestorians respectively. Their mentalities were diametrically opposed on many points, though they both were found among Syriac-speakers – perhaps they represent differences within that language. The Copts, who are the descendants of the ancient Egyptians, are also reckoned as Monophysites, though their views differ slightly from those of the Syrian Monophysites (or Jacobites). In all these groups the distinctive theological doctrines became the focus of the self-awareness of the group in their political opposition to the Byzantine Greeks. When they had been expelled from the Christian Church, they produced creeds which avoided the more serious heresies with which they had been charged. This was not sufficient, however, to bring about reconciliation, for a 'will to disunity' had come into being on both sides. Thus the exclusion of the oriental Christians from the Church and the councils on the ground of heresy led to their organization as separate communities distinct from the main body of Christians; and this weakened both the main body and the orientals.

For an adequate understanding of this expulsion of the orientals it is necessary to look at a wider background. Following the amazing conquests of Alexander the Great in the fourth century BC, there was a cultural expansion of Hellenism as far as the Oxus and North India. In the more easterly lands Hellenistic influence soon became weaker; but in the Persian (Sasanian) Empire in the time of Muhammad the dominant culture was Hellenistic in many respects. The Syriac-speaking Nestorians, expelled from the Byzantine Empire, had established institutions of higher learning in Iraq and other western parts of the Sasanian Empire. In these, though the language of instruction was Syriac, Greek philosophy and science (including medicine) were taught. Though progress had thus been made towards incorporating much Greek culture into the local

95

culture, it seems that there were some who still resented this culture and its association with Byzantine domination. If one begins from the other end and looks at Greek culture, one sees that much of this had been assimilated in Iraq, Syria and Egypt, so that they largely shared a common higher intellectual culture. The various ethnic and cultural groups in this area, however, had not fully come to terms with one another; and this discontent had political bearings. As already noted, theological doctrines became political slogans; and when the Muslims invaded Syria and Egypt, the inhabitants hailed them as liberators from the hated Greeks.

Some of these points have been summed up epigrammatically by Christopher Dawson in the words that Muhammad 'was the answer of the East to the challenge of Alexander'.[3] Muhammad was the originator of the Islamic state, and this new political entity, grown to the size of an empire, favoured indigenous culture against Hellenistic culture on the whole. The mentality of the Arabs was of course by no means identical with those of the peoples of Iraq and Syria, but it was closer to them than that of the Greeks, and under Islam they accepted much of it. The Christians, on the other hand, had been too much aligned with the diffusion of Hellenistic culture. Even after their expulsion from the Byzantine Empire the Nestorians were among the chief bearers of Hellenistic culture in Iraq. It was therefore not surprising that, when the reaction came against Greek culture, the Christians were among those who suffered. The situation is indeed comparable to the association of Christian missions during the last century and a half with the diffusion throughout the world of European-American culture. The whole world is accepting the scientific and technological aspects of our culture, but, as European colonialism recedes, it seems likely that many Christian footholds will be swept away, just as Hellenism lost ground before Islam.

Ultimately, it may be said, Christianity failed in the Middle East because it was unable to 'master' the environment.[4] Christianity was there confronted with a clash of cultures and peoples. There was the clash of various cultures within the Roman Empire; and there was the clash between the cultures within the empire and those beyond its eastern frontier. Christianity did much by way of reconciling the various groups of Greek-speakers to one another (that is, those who like many peoples of Asia Minor had no literary language other than Greek) and reconciling the Greek-speakers and the Latin-speakers. After the effort expended in achieving this, however, there was little energy left to deal adequately with the oriental Christians. Instead of making further efforts to appreciate their point of view and bring about a reconciliation, it was decided to take the easier course of branding them heretics. Some were forced to leave the Byzantine Empire and take refuge with the Sasanians. This was not only a disaster for the orientals expelled from the 'great church' and a weakening of the latter by the separation of many Christians. It led to a deterioration of the organism of Christianity, and a loss of the rich wholeness of truth.[5] The vision of Christian truth as seen by the Greeks, though only partial, was deemed to be absolute; and Christianity, at least in the eastern Mediterranean area and further east, was overmuch identified with the Greek dualistic outlook. Beyond a certain point Christianity had failed to bring harmony into the diversity.

In the precise area where Christianity failed, Islam succeeded. The lands once dominated by the oriental Christians are now solidly Muslim. In Asia Minor and European Turkey it may be that the original Christian inhabitants have mostly been driven out and replaced by others who were already or who soon became Muslims. Elsewhere, however, the descendants of oriental Christians often themselves became Muslims; and this must not be ascribed solely to materialistic and secular pressures, such as the fact that in Islamic states Christians were 'second-class citizens'. The Christian will only fully understand what happened if he is prepared to admit that here Christianity may have been inferior, perhaps even spiritually inferior. It is at least a plausible theory that the orientals became estranged somewhat from Christianity when the latter became overidentified with the Greek dualistic conception of man. By this is meant the view that a man consists of body and soul, and that the soul is the essential man, and the body only a garment or instrument of the soul, or even (as some extremists held) its tomb. On the other hand, among the oriental Christians and other peoples of the Middle East it would seem that some form of monistic conception of man was dominant. A distinction

G   97

might be made between body and soul, but the body was just as much the man as the soul, or more so. The monistic conception is illustrated in the New Testament in such passages as *Mark* 9.43-8 where it is said that it is better to enter into 'life' (that is, heaven) without a hand or foot or eye than to keep one's body intact and enter hell. Not only on this point but also on others the Nestorian mentality is close to that of the Muslim Arabs. It thus seems plausible to hold that among the oriental Christian peoples many became Muslims because they found in Islam an expression of monotheism more suited to their distinctive mentality than any provided by Christianity.

One might go still further and say that, while Christianity failed on the basis of Greek categories to provide for the oriental mentalities, Islam on the basis of Arab categories made some provision for Greek thought. It is a well-known fact that between the ninth and twelfth centuries much Greek science and philosophy was accepted into the intellectual milieu of Islam. It is interesting to notice now the Arabic word *nafs* has two distinct meanings. In the Qur'an it usually means 'self' in accordance with the monistic conception of man; but in writers influenced by Greek thought it means 'soul' (as opposed to body) in accordance with the dualistic conception. Not too much should be claimed in this matter, however, since there was much in Greek culture which Islam completely neglected, not least Greek tragedy, that great achievement of the poetic imagination. This neglect would seem to emphasize the point about the difference of mentalities.

3. The Formation of the Islamic World-view

Complementary to the fading-out of Christianity among those peoples of the Middle East who had been Christians was the elaboration of the Islamic world-view so that the Muslim intellectuals became the bearers of the intellectual culture of the whole area. To complete the picture of the influence of the Qur'anic revelation it is necessary to examine at least the chief stages in the working out of the world-view based on it.

The situation at the appearance of Islam was roughly as follows. In what became the Islamic heartlands there already was a certain cultural unity. This was especially so with Egypt, Syria, Iraq and Persia. They shared in the cultures developed in the Nile valley and that of the Tigris and Euphrates. With this had been fused something of Hellenistic culture, while Judaeo-Christian ideas had also permeated the whole. Abyssinia or Ethiopia also participated in this culture, though without the Hellenistic elements. Since Arabia lay on the fringe of this great culture area, it was inevitably influenced to some extent. The neighbours of Arabia on the north were the chief source of influence, but the Abyssinian occupation of the Yemen for about fifty years in the middle of the sixth century was a secondary source. From these sources Judaeo-Christian and Persian ideas made their way among the Arabs, though few traces of Hellenism are found. The presence of these ideas in the intellectual milieu into which the Qur'anic revelation came facilitated its later domination of the cultural area from which the ideas came.

Within the cultural area which became the heartlands of Islam the main cultural and intellectual focus was the Christian Church, or rather the 'great church'. By the sixth century this had its centre at Byzantium at the centre of the empire, and was of course concerned with a vastly wider area than the later Islamic heartlands. This gave more importance to various minor foci of intellectual life, such as the Copts in Egypt, the Jacobite Monophysites in Syria, the Nestorians chiefly in Iraq, Jews in Iraq and elsewhere, pagan philosophers in Harran. One of the results of the Arab conquests and the formation of the Islamic Empire was to cut off the Christian groups from the intellectual life of the Byzantine Empire. On the eve of the conquests they were already partly cut off by being regarded as heretics, but the creation of a new political frontier made the separation more effective. Nevertheless the minor Christian foci remained strong. The greatest missionary achievements of the Nestorians – their penetration of Central Asia and China – came after the Islamic conquest. The Greek philosophical schools too continued in some form for over two centuries. The vitality of all these foci, however, was less than that of the intellectual side of the Islamic religious movement.

Islam began with a 'will to unity' towards Jews and Christians. In other words, Muhammad would gladly have accepted them as members of his community, or perhaps even as associate members. In time, however, this 'will to unity' was changed into a 'will to disunity'; that is to say, Muhammad came to realize that it was necessary for his movement to retain its distinctive character and to avoid any assimilation to Judaism or Christianity. The 'will to disunity' was first manifested towards the Jews, as a result of the hostility shown to Muhammad by those in Medina, and led to the so-called 'break with the Jews' in 624. Fighting against Christian tribes on the route to Syria about 630 ruled out any possibility of a reconciliation between Muhammad and the Christians. These practical attitudes are reflected in, and are in part the outcome of, the Qur'anic conception of the religion of Abraham – that religion which is being restored in its pure form by the Muslims after having been corrupted by the Jews and Christians. Thus the 'will to disunity' was fully developed before the Muslims conquered the Christian populations of Syria, Egypt and Iraq. Islam was already asserting itself as independent of the two older religions and indeed as superior to them.

When to this pride in the superiority of their religion the Muslims added pride in their political and military superiority, the 'will to disunity' had placed impassable barriers between Muslims and Christians. The ordinary Muslim was protected by the doctrine of 'corruption' (*taḥrīf*) which meant in practice that, if a Christian wanted to argue with a Muslim, he had to do so on the Muslim's ground, since the doctrine asserted that the Bible was in some way corrupt, and so ruled it out of court as evidence. Some Muslim scholars, of course, had access to the Bible, especially after educated Christians and Jews were converted to Islam; and they accepted much material from it. They were careful in their selection, however, and neglected whatever was incompatible with the Qur'an.

While intellectual defences were thus being erected against Christianity and Judaism, many Muslim scholars were beginning to elaborate a distinctive world-view on a purely Arabic and Qur'anic basis. The new world-view arose from a combination of this attitude of self-sufficiency with certain practical needs. The Qur'an was used in worship and therefore had to be understood even by non-Arabs; and there was also a need for guidance in the settling of legal questions (in a wide sense) according to Islamic principles. To understand the Qur'an required a knowledge of grammar and lexicography. A grammatical science for the Arab language was worked out, chiefly at Basra in the second half of the eighth century. To determine the meaning of unusual words in the Qur'an scholars collected and wrote down the pre-Islamic poetry which had hitherto been transmitted orally. A proper understanding of the poetry further required some knowledge of the historical traditions of the pre-Islamic Arabs. Legal points, again, in the view of the more devout Muslims, ought to be decided on the basis of the legal rules found in the Qur'an supplemented, where necessary, by reference to the practice of Muhammad. Jurisprudence became the core of Islamic learning, and eventually was the centre of a group of scholarly disciplines. Besides jurisprudence proper (*fiqh*) there was a discipline known as 'principles of jurisprudence' (*uṣūl al-fiqh*). Then there was the study of the Traditions (in the technical sense of anecdotes about Muhammad) from which his standard practice might be inferred. Since unscrupulous men began to invent Traditions, various subordinate disciplines were developed which led to the formation of a corpus of 'sound Traditions'. In this way there was created a body of 'Islamic sciences' or 'disciplines' which jointly produced the Islamic world-view.

All these 'Islamic sciences' were elaborated out of Arabic and Qur'anic materials. When progress had been achieved in respect of these, however, some scholars felt able to tackle non-Arabic material. Points of Jewish or Christian teaching might be included in Traditions, which were often but not always considered spurious; for example, Muhammad was reported to have said that 'God created Adam in his image'. Similarly the brief Qur'anic references to Biblical stories were filled out from the Bible or from other Jewish or Christian books. The Biblical genealogies, especially of Abraham's ancestors and of his descendants through Ishmael, were linked up with the traditional Arab genealogies, thus giving the Arabs genealogies which stretched back to Adam. A different type of Muslim was attracted by Greek science and philosophy, as already noted in a different connection. Translations were made of Greek books, and then original works in Arabic were written. Among Muslim theologians the Mu'tazilites were early users of Greek conceptions in their apologetic writings. A further acceptance of Greek philosophy took place in the second half of the

eleventh century through al-Ghazālī; and from this time onwards Greek logic and certain metaphysical ideas were given a
fundamental place in much Islamic theology. Thus from about
the twelfth century onwards there was in being an Islamic
world-view, Qur'anic in essence, but with many elaborations
and additions, and this world-view became dominant in the
Islamic heartlands.

It might be objected that there was no imperative need for a
complete break with Judaism and Christianity, nor was it
necessary for a 'will to disunity' to emerge. In reply to this
objection it may be urged that such a break is often found in
human history. Thus the religion of the Israelites had to break
with Canaanite nature-religion, even though it was prepared
to take over many ideas and practices from it; and Islam had to
break with Meccan paganism. More generally it might be said
that a religion seems to require not merely patterns of thought
and conduct but also a centre or focus. Many of these patterns
were probably much the same for Nestorian Christians and for
Muslims, but the centre or focus was different and so the general
structure was different. The point might be put in a different
way by saying that in the historical organism of Middle East
culture there were for a time different foci, including the
Nestorian and the Islamic; but it appears to be a fact that in such
a historical organism there is a trend towards integration and
unity. The 'will to disunity' towards other groups is bound up
with the resolve that one's focus will be the one focus of the
whole historical organism, for in this case acceptance of the one
entails rejection of the other. Indeed the appearance of rival
foci in an organism can usually be only a temporary phenomenon. A strong and vigorous religion is bound to the main
focus of its historical organism. If one keeps in mind that there
is a close link between the concepts of focus and integration,
one can appreciate the remark of L. S. Thornton, thinking
chiefly of Christianity, that 'the creativity of revelation is
manifested in its capacity for integration of many cultures in
one traditional whole'.[6]

NINE

THE THEOLOGY OF REVELATION

☾

1. Islamic Doctrines of Revelation

The Qur'an speaks of itself as a message from God conveyed to Muhammad by angels, and in particular Gabriel. The message is conveyed to him so that he may communicate it to his fellow-Meccans in the first place. The implied picture appears to be of an important desert chief (in a society where writing is little cultivated) giving a message to a trusted servant to convey to someone at a distance; the message is naturally given by word of mouth. Sometimes the dramatic form of the Qur'an is that God speaks in his own person, often employing the plural of majesty. Sometimes the speaker is ostensibly the messenger, and he then refers to God in the third person. In Surat Maryam [19.64/5 f.] there are two curious verses beginning 'We come not down save by the command of thy Lord'; here the ostensible speakers are angels in the plural, though presumably God has told them to say what they say. In an earlier chapter (p. 14 above) a passage was quoted describing several different 'manners' of revelation, and these were spoken of as different ways in which God 'addressed' (*kallama*) a man. Thus it becomes appropriate that the message of God should be spoken of as his *kalām*, his 'address' or 'speech'. This word occurs four times in the Qur'an: once of the Bible or Old Testament [2.75/0], twice of the revelations to Muhammad [9.6; 48.15], and once in connection with God's addressing Moses [7.144/1]. This conception of the *kalām* of God is very similar to the Biblical conception of 'the word of God' (apart from the Christian identification of this with Jesus); but it is preferable to avoid the latter phrase, since in another Qur'anic passage [3.45/0; cf. 4.171/69] Jesus is spoken of as 'a word (*kalima*) from him (*sc.* God)'.

For at least a century and a half the Muslims appear to have accepted this phrase without being troubled by any intellectual difficulties. About 800, however, as already noted, the question began to be discussed whether the Qur'an was the uncreated speech of God, or whether it was a speech which he had created. Just how this question came to be raised is not altogether clear. Since the Qur'an was revealed at certain points in time, and since it refers to temporal events, it would have been natural to suppose that it was temporal and therefore created. On the other hand, if it really is the speech of God, it must somehow share in his eternity. The point at issue between the two parties would seem to be how fundamental the Qur'an is. Those who held it was uncreated seem to have wanted to say that the Qur'an was an expression of God's eternal being, whereas their opponents made it something dependent on his will, and therefore capable of being changed. Recent linguistic philosophy is prepared to speak of man as 'the being whose essence is . . . his "linguisticality"' since 'there is a deep affinity here between man and language'; and this may be applied to the word or speech of God.[1] In some way the Qur'an, as the speech of God, must be an expression of his eternal essence, whereas vast multitudes of created things are clearly not expressions of God's nature, and so there is no certainty that a created speech would express his essence, though it might be an illustration of his creative power.[2]

For those who held that the speech of God is uncreated, further problems presented themselves. One was connected with the unity of God. Upholders of the created Qur'an might argue that, if the Qur'an is the uncreated speech of God, we have two eternal and uncreated beings, God and his speech, and have therefore abandoned monotheism. It was probably as a result of discussions of this problem that a group of Muslim theologians developed their doctrine of the attributes of God. According to this doctrine God has various attributes — seven are often named, power, knowledge, life, will, speech, hearing, seeing — and these attributes are neither identical with his essence nor distinct from it. In other words, God's attributes in general and his speech in particular have a partly separate existence; they are neither identical with him nor separate from him; but the precise relationship cannot be described positively, but only indicated by these negatives.

Another problem is connected with the reciting or writing of the Qur'an. When one recites or writes it, sounds or marks on paper are made; and these sounds and marks must be labelled 'created' and not 'uncreated'. Since they are created, however, how is it possible for what we recite and write, and what others hear and read, to be the uncreated Qur'an? This problem is by no means peculiar to the Qur'an, though it is made more serious by the introduction of the ideas of created-ness and uncreatedness. When this book is printed by people I do not know and sold in shops in towns I have never visited, can I still be said to be addressing the reader? And if it is trans-lated into a language I do not know? Similarly, if we listen to a reproduction of the voice of some great singer of the past now dead, like Caruso or Kathleen Ferrier, do we really hear him or her singing? I should be inclined to say that we do. Ordinary hearing depends on the use of sound waves, but we say we hear the person. So why is it not the same when by using electricity and plastics we prolong the sound waves? It was probably something like this that the Muslim theologians had in mind when they tried to solve their problem by saying that what was recited, written, heard and read was not the eternal Qur'an, but a ḥikāya of it – perhaps we might translate here as 'repre-sentation'.

Yet another group of problems is connected with the references to historical events in the Qur'an. How can the Qur'an say that 'event x has happened' if the Qur'an is eternal? Event x happened at a particular point in time, and so before that point had been reached it was not true to say that 'event x has happened'. The same difficulty also occurs in respect of God's knowledge. His knowledge on Tuesday 'x will happen on Wednesday' is different from his knowledge on Thursday 'x happened on Wednesday'. This difficulty can be partly overcome by careful statement, in view of the fact that God's knowledge is above time in some sense. There would appear to be no logical contradiction in saying that God eternally knows the happening of event x on Wednesday 19 June AD 1963. That is to say, that part of the difficulty which comes from the temporal reference of verbs can be obviated by using the verbal noun which has no such temporal reference.

This does not completely dispose of the problem, however, for it is part of a wider one. Ultimately one is attempting to explain the relation of the eternal to the particularities of time, place, culture and the like. The problem is implicit in the phrase 'an Arabic Qur'an', since this presupposes some special relevance to the Arabian environment. There are, of course, in the Qur'an some perfectly general assertions, such as those about the signs in natural phenomena of God's power and goodness; but even these are formulated in terms of Arabic categories. In many other cases, however, the assertions of the Qur'an have a temporal reference, notably some of the novel assertions (as in Chapter 4), in which general principles are stated in a form specially applicable to Mecca and Medina in the early seventh century. As an example one might consider the command in 9.29, 'Fight against those who do not believe in God and the Last Day ... until they pay the *jizya* ...' Now one might regard it as a general principle that believers should fight against unbelievers until the latter submitted; so the particular command would be an application of the general principle to the circumstances of the Muslims towards the end of Muhammad's life. Yet the general principle itself has a temporal reference, since it is presumably only in this-worldly circumstances that such fighting will be necessary. It would therefore seem that much of the Qur'an is concerned with God's purposes for man's temporal life, whether these purposes are expressed in general principles applicable at all times, or are restricted to particular times and places. It follows that man is informed chiefly about God's temporal purposes, particular or general, and is told very little about the supratemporal aspects of God's being and knowledge. In other words, the eternal speech of God as known to man has mostly a temporal reference.

It would perhaps be not altogether fanciful to connect with this temporal reference of the Qur'an the fact that the messengers are always human beings and not angels.[3] Some of Muhammad's contemporaries seem to have thought that a messenger of God should be marked off in some way from the general run of men; for example, that he should not require to eat ordinary food, but should have a supernatural source of supply; per-

haps that an angel should always accompany him and serve
his needs.[4] This shows that the Qur'an is not merely God's
speech to men and for men, but that (though it comes from a
divine source) the later stages of its communication to men are
entirely human.

The Traditions, or anecdotes about Muhammad, are also
accepted as in some sense a part of revelation. This is implicit in
the community's acceptance of them as one of the bases of the
shari'a or revealed law. This whole attitude to the Traditions
might be explained by saying that Muhammad was the supreme
exemplar of the Islamic way of life, and had been consciously
accepted as such by the community, especially the Sunnite part
of it. Since the Islamic way of life is a response to revelation,
Muhammad's life and actions are in a sense a guide to his understanding of the revelation. This point can be made very effectively by bringing in the conception of organism. The people
who first respond to a revelation come to form a community
with special practices in worship and conduct, and these practices we call its religion. This is the beginning of the historical
organism. Later generations, however, respond to the revelation not in the isolated text of the revelation, but as the revelation is mediated by the religion of the community as practised
by the earlier generation.[5] Muslims have always given special
respect to the Companions of Muhammad, partly because they
were the witnesses to the sunna or standard practice of Muhammad, but also, in the case of some at least, because they themselves exemplified the Islamic way of life. It is to the words and
actions of Muhammad above all, however, that Muslims ascribe
this revelatory function, namely, the interpretation in actual
practice and response of the original revelation.

This interdependence of revelation and the community is to
be emphasized. It does not, of course, reduce the element of
divine initiative in the revelation, but shows that the revelation
is always given to people who will respond, whether the
response be positive or negative. According to the Qur'an
revelation is always carried by a messenger to a 'people', that
is, a body of human beings (or other spiritual beings). If the
recipients of the message respond positively, a religious community is formed. The discussions about the uncreatedness
of the Qur'an showed that many Muslims were aware of the

fundamental place of the Qur'an in the life of their community. The Qur'an is, as it were, the backbone of the historical organism of Islam, which gives it a fixed structure. On the other hand, however, the community is in some sense a part of the revelation – an embodiment of it, through which the revelation continues to act so that future generations are faced with the decision to respond or not to respond. Neither the Qur'an nor any other scripture is likely to be effective except when it is associated with a community. It might at first sight seem that the Black Muslim movement in the United States is an exception to this; the leaders seem to have called themselves Muslims on the basis of a very slight knowledge of Islam and no real contact with the Islamic community. Yet even here it would seem that one of the things which attracted them was the anti-European attitude which had often been present and 'embodied' in the historical community of Muslims.

This consideration of the theology of revelation in Islam has imperceptibly led to the raising of questions, which, though they are still about revelation in Islam, presuppose various modern and contemporary interests. It is therefore appropriate to pass to an explicitly modern review of the questions connected with revelation in general and Islamic revelation in particular.

2. A 'Modern' Account of Revelation

The development of the natural or empirical sciences with their great practical triumphs is a factor which has done much to form the 'modern' mentality in Europe and America, and indeed throughout the world. One of the features of this mentality is its concern for actual experience. Accordingly these reflections begin from a consideration of Muhammad's experience as human experience. So far as can be told from the records the essential feature of this experience was that he found certain words in his heart or consciousness. Normally there was no accompanying vision, but only the words. The belief that the words had been brought by an angel does not appear to have been part of the primary experience, though it might be called a secondary experience. To these words which came into his heart Muhammad responded positively. He also communicated them to his friends and other persons, and they likewise responded. In this way the Islamic community was formed.

The question now frames itself: How did these words, which constituted the primary experience, come into Muhammad's consciousness? We accept his sincerity in holding that they were not the result of any conscious thought-processes. For a 'modern' the easy answer is that the words came from Muhammad's unconscious. This answer, however, is little more than a reformulation of the question. All it adds is that the words were somehow related to Muhammad before he became consciously aware of them. This point might be combined with traditional Islamic views by holding that the angel placed the words in an aspect of Muhammad's being called the 'unconscious', and that from this they emerged into consciousness. One might even say that the unconscious is the sphere in which angels (and demons) are operative. A responsible Christian theologian has suggested that the modern equivalent for 'evil spirit' is unconscious complex.[6] All this amounts to saying that some further account of the unconscious is required.

The view to be adopted here is in the main the Jungian one. According to this view what emerges from the unconscious into consciousness in dreams and fantasies of individuals and also in the religious myths of a whole community comes from the libido or life-energy which is the spring of activity in all men. In an individual man the libido is in part something particular to himself and in part something he shares with the other members of his community and ultimately with the whole human race. This part which is shared with other men is called by Jung the 'collective unconscious'. To the working of the collective unconscious are ascribed much religious myth and also dogma, especially the figures like 'the hero', 'the leader', 'the divine child', 'the virgin', which are found in many religions. In the contemplation and worship of these figures a man may find that there is a release of psychical energy within him, which gives him the power to accomplish what would otherwise be impossible for him. In short, according to the Jungian scheme, most religious ideas emerge from the collective unconscious into consciousness, and most religious practice is the conscious response to these ideas.

According to this way of looking at the matter, the revelations on which Judaism, Christianity and Islam are based are
'contents' which have emerged from the collective unconscious. There is a great variety and complexity in these contents. Among the Old Testament prophets a prominent place
is taken by certain figures or images; God is spoken of as the
shepherd or husband of his people; men are taught to look for
the coming of the Messiah, the divinely-inspired king who will
deliver his people from their troubles. The prophets take their
place within a continuing tradition – the historical organism of
Israelite religion – and part of their work is to develop further
the images already accepted by the people. The work of Jesus
was similar, in that he carried some of the images of the Jewish
religion a stage onwards. In particular he claimed that he was
the expected Messiah, but he combined this with the image of
the 'suffering servant' and with ideas of sacrifice, and then
deliberately set about 'living out' these ideas. In Muhammad,
who lived in a region only slightly influenced by Judaeo-
Christian ideas, there was a sudden and largely unprepared-for
emergence of contents from the collective unconscious.

Some readers may be horrified and many more may feel
uneasy at the suggestion that revelations come from the
collective unconscious. Such a reaction is unjustified and due to
a misunderstanding. The suggestion just made is concerned
only with a proximate explanation, not with the ultimate explanation. The essential points it makes are two: that most
religious ideas come from the same source in men and that this
source is a part or aspect of the life-energy. It remains open to a
religious man to hold that God works through this collective
unconscious. It is commonly asserted by religious people that
their 'daily bread' or *rizq* ('provision') comes from God; this
would be the ultimate cause or explanation, though God is
often spoken of as acting directly without any intermediate
causes. The same people, however, are fully aware of the
labours of farmers, millers, bakers, shopkeepers and others
through which their food comes to them, as well as of the
influence of physical causes like the weather; these are proximate
causes yielding only a proximate explanation. The religious
man speaks of God giving him his daily bread, despite the
intermediate cause. In the same way may he not speak of God

revealing things to him and addressing him, although there may be intermediate causes like the collective unconscious?

The suggested view, then, is that God, the transcendent source of all being, works through the collective unconscious. Such terms as 'source' and 'works through' are, of course, diagrammatic. One of the primary meanings of 'source' is where a river takes its beginning from a spring bubbling out of the earth. Again, a business man may work through an agent, or a body of people may work through an executive committee. Thus these terms express diagrammatically one aspect of the relation of the transcendent to the temporal, or, more precisely, the relation of that which transcends time and space to that which is part of the spatio-temporal process. It is a moot point whether the collective unconscious in any way transcends the spatio-temporal process, but it is certainly known chiefly through its operations in the process. Since it is always difficult for the human mind to express the relation of the eternal and transcendent to the temporal, one may ask whether this dia-gram of that relationship is markedly less successful than others. May it not even be more successful in that it expresses the relationship in concepts akin to those in which modern occi-dental man normally thinks?

It is also to be noted that there is an element of creativity in the collective unconscious, and this makes it further appropri-ate as the agent of the transcendent source of being. The collective unconscious is an aspect of the functioning of the life-energy in men; and the life-energy is the principle of life in them – that by which they live. It is the life-energy which causes the embryo to develop in the womb of the mother, and leads the child to develop its latent powers. When life for an individual or community has become unsatisfactory in some respect it is the life-energy which causes 'contents' or ideas to emerge from the unconscious of some person. In so far as these ideas are from the collective unconscious, and are not peculiar to the individual, they will meet with a response from other members of the community, and in favourable circumstances a religious movement will be born. The collective unconscious thus functions creatively to bring a community to a fuller and more satisfactory experience. The life-energy and the collective unconscious are also creative in the sense that man is their creature. They make man what he is, but he has no ultimate control over them. For all of us the stream of life flows irresistibly on, whether we will or no; and the most we can achieve is a little steering, as of a canoe in a fast current. The suicide of an individual only means the submergence of his canoe or the disintegration of his bundle of consciousness; but the stream of life continues. Even if the human race destroys most of itself with nuclear bombs, the stream of life will continue, though it may be switched into a different evolutionary channel.

When we try to observe the functioning of the life-energy, we are unable to go back to an absolute beginning, but have to be content to commence our observations at a middle-point in the process. This is no great disadvantage, however, since it is a feature of life to move forward from the point already reached. This should be obvious, but is worth stating explicitly. During the next hour the life in me will function on the basis of what my past life has made me, physically, psychically, intellectually and in every other way. Similarly when ideas emerge from the collective unconscious, though there is an element of novelty in them, they are not a complete break with the past, but a development of what is already present. This was certainly the case with the Old Testament prophets. The novel assertions which emerged through them from the collective unconscious were often an expansion, modification or partial revision of ideas which had emerged previously and been accepted by the community. The novel assertions were required either because the community had somehow distorted the ideas or (perhaps more often) because new circumstances had arisen in which fresh guidance was required. It would seem that the same also holds of the creative irruption or emergence of ideas in the Qur'anic revelation. It was appropriate in the first place to the people of Mecca and Medina in the time of Muhammad, giving them guidance in the particular situation in which they then were – though it also met the fundamental needs of men in other situations. The novel assertions of the Qur'an, too, were made in terms of the categorial, cosmological, historical and other presuppositions of the people of Mecca and Medina.

The general point just made could also be expressed by saying that the unconscious always speaks to men in terms of what is already in their consciousness. This could further be taken as an instance of the law that the unconscious, even the collective unconscious, in working through a man does not violate his personality. When contents from the collective unconscious emerge in him, he does not cease to be himself, just as, when someone in authority speaks to him, he does not cease to be himself, though he has to decide whether to obey or disobey. In other words, the ideas from the collective unconscious do not *compel* a man to do anything; they do not change him into a machine. They function as one factor in his make-up along with others. If they override the others, they do so only in ways in which it is appropriate for one such factor to override others. The truly human personality is preserved and not violated.

It may be claimed, then, that this 'modern' view of the nature of revelation can be harmonized with all the points in the traditional doctrine that are of practical importance to the religious man, and, further, that it is not incompatible with theism. What has been said here is, of course, far from being a complete discussion of all the problems. The greatest of all, how the transcendent source of our being is related to the collective unconscious, has been left virtually untouched. Yet sufficient has perhaps been said to show that the doctrine of revelation can be meaningfully treated in a 'modern' context.

TEN

ISLAM IN THE FUTURE WORLD

ؤ

1. The Present Relation of Islam to Christianity

Under the Roman Empire there was a certain cultural unity from Britain to Syria, though within this culture there were sub-cultures differing greatly from one another. The cultural regions occupied by these sub-cultures overlapped somewhat. For present purposes the most important distinction is between Latin culture, Greek culture and 'oriental' culture; of these the first was that of western Europe, the second that of the eastern Mediterranean, while the third – closely linked with the 'oriental' Christian churches – dominated some of the eastern provinces of the Roman Empire and was akin to the culture of the Euphrates and Tigris valley. Gradually Christianity became identified with Latin and Greek culture, while the culture of the 'oriental' Christians, after they had been dubbed heretics, was eventually absorbed by the historical organism of Islam. In the course of time the cultural regions ceased to overlap and became distinct from one another.

This separateness has been broken down during the last century or two. The whole world indeed has been culturally unified at the material level by modern science and technology. The world is still many, however, on the basis of the great religio-cultures of the past and the corresponding cultural regions, since these have not yet been much affected by the unification of material culture. On the contrary there has been what is usually called a resurgence of the world religions, though it could also be said that in view of the growth of the scientific mentality the religions have ceased to control the cultures with which they are associated. In some respects the whole world faces the same problems; but the cultural regions associated with Christianity and Islam not merely have modern material culture in common, but are also both inheritors of the intermingled cultures of the Roman Empire. The Jewish element in Christian culture is close to the 'oriental' culture of the Roman Empire while Islamic culture borrowed much from Greek logic, metaphysics and science. In the course of the centuries the cultures of Christendom and Dar al-Islam each became relatively homogeneous, but diverged more from one another. This affinity raises special problems. On the one hand it may facilitate a measure of understanding; but on the other hand the contacts of the two religions during the early formative period have given each strong intellectual defences against the other. This combination of hostility and affinity gives a special urgency to the dialogue between Christendom and Islam.

The association of a religion with a cultural region makes it impossible to compare religions objectively in respect of truth. Each cultural region has its own categories of thinking, its own historical consciousness, and its own world-view. These have taken a definitive shape gradually through the centuries under the integrative pressure of the religion. The Islamic mentality of the heartlands is based primarily on the Arab mentality of the early seventh century, but it has also incorporated something of the Greek intellectual outlook and the 'oriental' Christian historical consciousness (based on the Old Testament). In time the varieties of mentality which originally existed became assimilated to the dominant mentality. Thus there took place a symbiosis of this culture we call Islamic with the religion of Islam. For one who has lived wholly within this culture especially in the heartlands, Islam is bound to appear absolutely true, and every other religion partly or entirely false. The position, of course, has been altered slightly by the intrusion of the scientific outlook. A similar symbiosis has taken place between Christianity and the culture of Europe and North America, though the development in these regions of the scientific outlook has made the situation more complex. Yet it remains true that for those brought up as Christians within this culture Christianity is bound to appear much nearer the truth than any other religion. The same holds of each of the great world-religions in its associated cultural region.

It is impossible, however, to maintain that the criteria of

truth used, say, by Christianity are superior to those used by Islam. The criteria of truth depend partly on categorial assumptions and partly on assumed valuations. In particular Christians exaggerate the importance of historicity, and can point, for example, to the unhistorical character of the Qur'anic account of the visit of Abraham to Mecca. This emphasis on historicity, however, has as its complement a neglect of the truth of symbols; and it may be that ultimately 'symbolic truth' is more important than 'historical truth'. Thus the criticisms of Islam by Christianity and of Christianity by Islam, though acceptable to Christians and Muslims respectively in the sense of appearing objectively true, would in neither case appear to be objective to a genuinely impartial observer. In other words, there is no way in the present situation of objectively comparing one of the great religions with another. It is relatively easy to give the adherents of one religion apparently objective reasons for holding their religion superior to others; but these reasons will appear weak and prejudiced to the adherents of the other religions because they are not in terms of the religio-cultural context of their lives. For the immediate future there is no escape from this impasse, so we must in humility learn to live with it.

There is, however, a way forward. The process of symbiosis between a religion and a cultural region, in the course of which the cultural region acquired a basic homogeneity, is likely to be repeated on a world scale. The expansion of the scientific outlook through the world is a starting point for the process. As each religio-culture comes to terms with the scientific outlook, it *ipso facto* comes closer to the other religio-cultures; and in this way there will be a slow movement towards a homogeneous culture for the world. In such a culture an objective comparison of religions will be possible. In the course of the development of the homogeneous culture, however, the issues between the religions will probably have largely solved themselves. In a sense one can already compare religions on the basis of the principle 'by their fruits you shall know them' [*Matthew*, 7.16]; but the assessment of 'fruits' is affected by the cultural background of the person making the judgement. It would seem, however, that the 'fruits' to be chiefly considered by anyone comparing religions during the next few decades will be such things as the ability to adapt traditional forms and ideas to contemporary circumstances and the ability to incorporate the values realized in other religions.

This argument could be summed up by saying that at present and for the visible future it is necessary to acknowledge a certain 'complementarity' of the great religions. Each is valid in a particular cultural region, but not beyond that. None has yet shown itself valid in all cultural regions, despite Christian, Islamic and other missionary movements. Since, then, each religion is valid in a particular cultural region, the religions complement one another in that each in a particular region enables men to live a good life.

2. Mission and Dialogue

In the light of the above analysis of the contemporary situation it would seem that missionary work as understood by European and American Christians in the nineteenth and early twentieth centuries is no longer possible, except perhaps in some isolated cases. To understand why this should be so it will be useful to look at some cases of successful missionary work in the past, and to try to discover the reasons for the successes. The first great missionary expansion of Christianity was that in the Roman Empire in New Testament times led by Paul and the other apostles. Broadly speaking, this expansion took place in a region where the culture was more or less similar. Paul's chief successes were among the urban populations where there had already been some intermingling of Greek and 'oriental' culture. Many of Paul's most devout converts came from the ranks of 'those who feared God', that is, from Gentiles attracted by Jewish teaching and worship, but unwilling to adopt the Jewish law in its entirety, partly no doubt because they did not want to become members of the segregated Jewish communities. Thus the spread of Christianity into Asia Minor and Europe was largely among persons who shared with Paul in citizenship of the Roman empire and in a degree of familiarity with Greek intellectual culture, while at the same time they were attracted by certain Jewish religious ideas. In so far as there was any crossing of culture barriers it took place when Paul became a Christian with his combination of Judaism and Greek intellectual culture.

The expansion of Christianity in western Europe must be seen in its relation to the Roman Empire. There is first of all an expansion within the Empire, following on the acceptance of Christianity by many persons in the capital, Rome. The decline of the western empire and its disintegration under the impact of the barbarian invasions led to some recession of Christianity; but after a time Christianity was found to meet the needs both of peoples who had formerly been within the empire and of those who, without being in the empire, had been influenced by Roman culture. Apart from Christianity there was no religion among the barbarian invaders or their subjects which was capable of sustaining men's sense of values in the chaos of the times. Where Christianity spread in western Europe, then, the different cultures might be regarded as variants of a single pattern.

The expansion of Christianity through the missionary efforts of the nineteenth and early twentieth centuries had some points of similarity with that earlier expansion, but there were also significant points of difference. The connection of the earlier expansion with the spread of Roman culture was paralleled by its connection in the nineteenth century with the spread of European culture. The chief successes of the missionary movement were among peoples with a relatively simple culture, especially where there was no highly organized religion to support it. In many parts of Africa, for example, where the local culture was breaking down, Africans accepted almost as part of the same process both the white man's technology (including education) and the white man's religion.

More important, however, are the differences between the recent expansion and the original expansion into western Europe. The recent missionary movement also attempted to penetrate the cultural regions of the world dominated by the higher religions. The inhabitants of these regions also wanted European technology and material culture; but at the same time many of them had a deep loyalty to their religion which they felt to be superior to that of the Europeans. Thus the successes of the Christian missionary movement in these regions were extremely limited. Most of the converts came from groups on the periphery of the culture or with an unsatisfactory social position within the culture. The intellectual and spiritual leaders

118

of the great religions, however, were virtually untouched, except that some of them became aware of Christianity as a challenge to their religious system, and took steps to meet the challenge. In these alien cultural regions, then, Christianity has hardly begun to get a foothold. This is especially true of the Islamic cultural region.

This does not mean, of course, that the great world religions remain static. Far from it. Apart from the Christian missionary movement all the great cultural regions have to meet that series of challenges often called 'the impact of the West'. The basic factor is the spread of European technology, not least the improvement of communications. This leads on to involvement in some branch of the world economic system, and then to political involvement. Again, men have to be trained to use the European inventions, and this exposes them to the scientific outlook. Thus the resurgence of the world religions is not simply a defence to the attack on their positions by the Christian missionary movement, but a response to the vast challenge presented by a whole series of economic, social, political and intellectual experiences.

While this has been happening to the world religions, there has been a certain warping of missionary motives among Christians. Perhaps some warping was present throughout the nineteenth century along with a degree of confusion between the achievements of Christianity and those of European civilization. Certainly after the First World War there seems to have been an increase among the supporters of Christian missions of the spirit of proselytization, though this is denounced in the New Testament (*Matthew*, 23.15). The proselytizing spirit enters in when the focus of attention is no longer the men and women with needs which can be relieved, but the prosperity – often in a material sense – of the Christian community, the church. This can be documented in various ways. There are such phrases as 'the conquest of the world for Christ'. There is the interest in missionary statistics, especially the number of converts and the growth in the membership of the local churches. On this last point there is a striking contrast with Islam. Although Islam is reckoned a missionary religion, there is little boasting in it about converts. The attitude seems rather to be that the Islamic community is doing such persons a favour by accepting them as brothers. Such an attitude can only spring from a deep confidence in the truth of one's religion – a confidence that does not require to be bolstered by statistics. The occidental Christians, on the other hand, are passing through a crisis of self-confidence. They have seen whittled away that material and political pre-eminence of Europe on which their forerunners prided themselves; and they have not sufficiently come to terms with the scientific outlook. Where the missionaries are uncertain, there are unlikely to be many satisfactory converts.

In the contemporary situation, then, missions as understood at the end of the nineteenth century are no longer possible, apart from some exceptional cases. In most areas, too, the 'foreign' missionary is no longer required as such, since there is a local Christian community capable of assuming responsibilities, including that for the evangelization of their fellows. Actually many of those who are still being sent abroad from Europe or North America are now looked upon as serving the 'indigenous' church. Thus 'traditional' methods are already virtually abandoned, and in particular the principle of sending paid agents to lands of alien culture with the primary aim of proclaiming a religious message and seeking to gain adherents to their religion. Those who still go abroad as 'missionaries' are in fact doing specific jobs for an institution already established in the country to which they go. The whole conception of 'foreign missions' is thus being replaced by one of mutual help between Christian communities in different parts of the world.

A new conception has also been applied to the relations of the religions, namely, that of 'dialogue'. This is understood, however, in many different ways. For some it would seem to be a matter of high-powered conferences, perhaps ending in agreed statements. For others the idea seems rather to be, say, that a number of Christian and Muslim theologians have a series of meetings at which they consider rival formulations of doctrinal principles; and then in due course they will all reach the conclusion that some of these propositions are true and others false. Yet others speak of 'dialogue' where the element of mutuality is at a minimum – like a Swiss writer who concluded a book entitled *Dialogue with Islam* with the following appeal to Muslims:

'We ask you very specially, you who so boldly assert the
kinship of our two religions, to entertain the thought
that the West has something more and better to give
you than its culture, its capital and its genius for inven-
tion: a Word of Life, a vision of the Kingdom of God,
and an infinite hope expressed in one word, one name,
Jesus Christ.'[1]

This is not dialogue in any important sense. This sentence
would convey nothing even to a well-educated Muslim; and
if he should perceive something of its meaning, he would simply
reply that he already has a superior word of life in the Qur'an,
and that he believes that God will in his good time establish
righteousness on the earth.

If the point is kept in mind that the type of dialogue relevant
here is that between persons from different cultural regions, it
will be seen that dialogue desiderates a high degree of openness
to what the other man is saying. There can be no dialogue of
any kind unless the one party listens to what the other party is
saying and in some measure understands it. This is particularly
difficult between alien cultures, because of the factors already
mentioned such as categorial differences. If a Christian and a
Muslim are merely seeking arguments against one another, they
will easily find many; but this will not lead to dialogue. For
dialogue there must first of all be a willingness to learn; and
across cultures this means great patience in familiarizing oneself
with all the aspects of the strange mentality. Only after a long
process of this kind will a man be able to listen with adequate
appreciation when the other speaks. In the process of becoming
familiar with the other mentality, however, the man will also
have become more open. As he appreciates the values of the
other religion he will begin to wonder whether there is any way
in which he can incorporate these values in his own religion.
The Christian author just quoted was very courteously en-
couraging Muslims to consider whether they could not, without abandoning the main part of their tradition, add something
to it; but he failed to see that he, as a Christian, should have been
asking himself whether Islam had anything to offer – perhaps
the deep trust in God of the average Muslim – which he should
have been trying to add to his Christianity.

It would further seem necessary for true dialogue that each participant should distinguish between the kerygma or positive message of his religion and its defences. By defences are meant the assertions and arguments by which a religion prevents its adherents from being unsettled by criticisms and contrary assertions made by adherents of other religions. The defences may be statements about particular matters or interpretations of texts. Rival interpretations of texts are mostly found where different sects of a religion accept the same scriptures. An important part of the defences of a religion is the assertion that in specified respects other religions are weak and bad and that it is strong and good. Thus Old Testament religion asserts that it is superior to the Canaanite religion because it worships God who is real and living, whereas the Canaanite worships alleged deities which are only pieces of wood and stone. Now the modern religious man may agree that Israelite religion was superior to Canaanite, but he would not consider the reason just quoted a sound one, since it fails to do justice to the positive values of Canaanite religion, some of which, as noted above, were eventually given a central place in Israelite religion and in Christianity. The assertion about worshipping wood and stone was a defence, intended primarily to discourage Israelites from taking any part in Canaanite ceremonies, and such discouragement was doubtless necessary for a time. The assertion, however, is a distortion, and not strictly true, for the Canaanites really worshipped natural powers symbolized by the wood and stone.

A religion's defences always include an element of distortion and exaggeration, especially with regard to the other religions with which it has been chiefly in contact. Christianity in its formative period had to defend itself against Judaism. This was chiefly done by claiming that Christians had a superior interpretation of the Old Testament. At a later period the view came to be popularly held that the Jews as a whole were responsible for the death of Jesus; and the Second Vatican Council has recently admitted that this is a distortion and tried to correct it. The Christian defences against Islam included the beliefs that Muhammad was a conscious impostor, that Islam pandered to man's sexual lusts, and that Islam had made converts solely by military force. Islam has its defences against Judaism and

Christianity, notably its assertion of the corruption of their scriptures. It is hardly too much to say that, wherever a religion compares itself with another, there is distortion and a measure of falsehood both in what it says about itself and in what it says about the other. This is so even with that final citadel of defence, 'My religion is the final religion, superior to all others, and containing the central truths about the universe and man's life.'

If there is to be genuine dialogue, then each side must abandon its defences. In the dialogue with Islam Christians must abandon the view that Muhammad was an impostor and similar views. 'But surely,' it will be said by Christian and Muslim alike, 'I cannot abandon the idea that my religion is superior to others; I am bound to believe my religion is superior, since otherwise I ought to leave it for the one I considered superior.' Such a statement is full of misapprehensions. Men do not leave one religion for another after an objective assessment of their respective merits, but usually because the adherents of the new religion seem to be able to do something for them – often at a worldly level – which the adherents of the old were unable to do. Then there is the conviction, on which much of the argument of this book is based, that at the present time it is impossible to compare religions with genuine impartiality. No one can know both Christianity and Islam adequately from the inside; a convert from one to the other is unlikely, because of his personal experiences, to be able to give an un-biassed account. For a similar reason no one can objectively compare the 'fruits' of the two religions. It may be suggested by someone that the doctors of the past, whose authority helped to form the image of the other religion, had good reasons for what they said. To this the rejoinder may be given that the authoritative doctors of the past had no fuller knowledge of the other religion than is open to the modern adherent, and were therefore in no position to make a valid objective comparison. In short, no one is justified in saying, 'My religion is better than yours'. What he may say, and indeed is bound to say, is, 'This is the positive message of my religion, and I believe it is true'.

Since no comparison of religions, that is, no assessment of them in terms of superiority and inferiority, can be objectively valid, the spirit of true dialogue demands that such comparisons be avoided. This applies even to latent comparisons, as when one says, 'My religion is the final religion', since 'final' here implies 'superior to others' or 'superseding others'. The desirability of avoiding such comparisons is reinforced by the teaching of modern psychology which sees in assertions of one's superiority a sign of weakness. If a man is really convinced of the truth of his beliefs, he does not need to give them further support by asserting their superiority to others. A religious community which asserts that its beliefs are superior to those of other communities may feel it is necessary to do this for the sake of its weaker members; but to do so is still a sign of weakness and an admission of the existence of 'weak' members. Many lines of thought, then, make it clear that, if we are to have true dialogue with members of other religions, indeed if we are to live in genuine involvement with the world around us, we must abandon this ultimate citadel of defence – the belief that our religion is superior to others.

At first sight many people will think that the abandonment of their defences is tantamount to the abandonment of their religion. Most emphatically this is not the case. Rather it is the abandonment of a false emphasis in their religion and the recovery of the true emphasis, namely, the basing of one's life on the positive truths of one's religion. After the abandonment of the specious defences, a man has greater opportunities of asserting the kerygma of his religion. This is indeed both mission and dialogue. It is a return to the earliest form of Christian mission. The great apostle Paul was seldom a 'paid agent', for he preferred to earn his own living by the secular trade of tent-making [cf. *Acts*, 18.3; 2 *Thessalonians*, 3.8]. In this way Paul shared the secular life of people before he spoke to them about religious matters. To this conception modern Christians and others are returning. Mission is seen to be the activity of a man who does a useful piece of work in the world (other than proclaiming religious truths), but who chooses to do this in a sphere where he is exposing himself to an alien religious culture and familiarizing himself with it. The Little Brothers of Jesus (the order founded by Charles de Foucauld) engage in humble manual work among poor people in non-Christian countries. Others contribute to developing countries by their educational, industrial or agricultural skills. In the process of doing this they are sharing the lives of the members of the alien religion and culture. Their own lives are open to inspection, and all may see how far their religion enables them to cope with the problems common to the milieu. This is the witness of a life. It allows all to see the 'fruits' of a man's religion in his life, which is not a special form of life but a shared common life.

The witness of a shared life is the primary aspect of mission. Where this witness is being made satisfactorily, however, there is a place for the witness of words in the form of the assertion of positive truths. The person who has shared in the life of an alien culture, however, has been familiarizing himself with the thought-forms of that religio-culture. He is therefore better able to express the truths of his own religion in a form that the others will appreciate. He has also no doubt been beginning to respond religiously to some of the beliefs of the other religion, and been trying to incorporate them into his own religious practice. This would seem to be the form which both religion and dialogue will take in the immediate future.

It is perhaps worth pointing out that engagement in dialogue often has a further result, namely, to induce a more sophisticated attitude towards all religion. It is noteworthy that in Islamic Spain, where Muslims, Christians and Jews were intermingling, there appeared a philosophical form of the Islamic religion, whose chief representatives were Ibn-Ṭufayl and Ibn-Rushd (or Averroes). In effect these men held that the true expression of religion was the philosophical one, and that the popular Islam of the masses was the nearest approximation to the true religion of which ordinary men were capable. They did not discuss the other religions explicitly, but some of their writing suggests that they regarded popular Christianity and popular Judaism as similar approximations to the true religion, though less successful than popular Islam. Something similar is implied by the preceding paragraphs. Since all religions may be improved by incorporating in them the values of other religions, all are approximations to the true religion, and none is yet complete. Some may be better approximations than others but objective comparison on this point is impossible. A modern man would not identify the true religion with a philosophical one, but would rather assert that it lies beyond the grasp of the

human intellect, at least for the present. It can be grasped partially and in vague outline, but not wholly and in detail. Men can
also move towards a fuller grasp of it. The true religion in its
perfection, however, will probably always be beyond man's
full comprehension in this mundane life.

3. The Acceptance of Complementarity

It is time to recapitulate some of the points that have been
made and try to reach a conclusion. The world has now been
materially unified on the basis of occidental science and technology, but it is far from being unified in other respects. The great
religio-cultures retain their vitality, as can be seen by the
resurgence of the religions in recent times. All are engaged in
dialogue with the scientific outlook, and will probably maintain themselves to some extent against it, since a purely scientific
outlook cannot meet all man's deeper needs. The life-energy is
bound to burst out of the strait-jacket of the scientific outlook.
At the same time the great religions are all engaged in the
searching task of adapting themselves to the contemporary
situation created by the technological developments. In this
direction it may well be that the achievements of some religions
will be greater than those of others. Thus at the present time all
the religions have in common both the dialogue with science
and the need for adaptation to technological culture. Nevertheless the religions, despite this sharing of life, will still find communication difficult, and advance in dialogue will be slow. For
many decades to come, then, the great religions will go on side
by side. Each is moderately successful within its own religio-
culture, and therefore they will have to learn to accept one
another as complementary, at least for the time being.

This situation of complementarity, if the word be allowed,
has to be looked at from a theological standpoint. The Christian likes to use such phrases as 'the purpose of creation' and
'the true order of human life', and supposes that these have
been fully made known to man in the Bible. In view of what
has been said above this supposition must now be abandoned
as a 'defence' – at least if the inference is made that these matters
are less fully made known by other religions. The phrases,
however, remain; and as soon as one reflects, it is clear that the
different religio-cultures must have been part of the purpose

and plan of creation. They are different ways in which the life-energy is working towards its purposes, different experiments aimed at attaining fulness of life in mundane conditions. Each great religion must be based in some sense on a divine revelation, for each has been more or less successful – shows satisfactory 'fruits' – in the particular conditions and circumstances in which it developed. Over a wide area each great religion has produced a measure of homogeneity at the intellectual and spiritual level – here indicated by the term 'religio-culture'. Because of the symbiosis of each religion with the associated religio-culture the religions cannot be validly compared with one another. Consequently so long as the associated cultures remain distinct, the religions will continue to be complementary, since each expresses in terms suited to the mentality of a particular culture the truths about the nature of the universe and of human life.

In the long term, of course, it is to be expected that there will be one religion for the whole world, though it may contain within itself permitted variations, comparable to the four permitted legal rites (*madhāhib*) in Sunni Islam. It would appear, however, that a movement towards religious unity is unlikely to proceed very far unless it follows on or is accompanied by a movement towards cultural unity. Such a movement may indeed be said to have already begun, and there are secular pressures urging it onward. Even in the different religio-cultures the basis of much of men's thinking is a common scientific one. Because of this men will feel bound to aim at a common categorization of the other, more directly religious, aspects of their experience. This pressure alone, however, is unlikely to produce a true unity, since it will tend to cease when a superficial unity has been attained. True unity will come rather as a by-product from a concern with more urgent tasks. The most urgent of all tasks for each religion is the adaptation of itself to contemporary circumstances. What men want and need most from a religion at the present time is guidance and strength to live in this world of mass-producing technological industry, rapid communications and material unification, with all the tensions to which these factors lead. They also need to be shown how to deal intellectually with the challenge of the scientific outlook. This adaptation will doubtless come about in various ways; but however it comes about, it will make it easier for men to cope with the problems they meet in daily living. By their 'fruits' of this kind the religions will be judged.

Since in this future world many men will have frequent contacts with those belonging to alien religio-cultures, they will tend, wherever one religion has made a valuable advance in adaptation, to try to incorporate this advance in the other religions. In this attempt some religions will be more successful than others. The religion which is most successful in incorporating the values of other religions into itself and genuinely integrating them with its essential vision, is most likely to gain converts from the other religions. Other men will appreciate the 'fruits' of a successful adaptation in the lives of the adherents of the religion making it. They will first try to achieve something similar in their own religion; but, if the result is not satisfactory, they will transfer their allegiance to the other religion. Thus the mentality – in its developed form – associated with this latter religion will tend to oust other mentalities, and progress will be made towards a homogeneous world mentality. On the basis of such a mentality some objective comparison of religions will be possible.

Most Christians tend to assume that the eventual religion of the whole world will be Christianity; but this is far from certain. To mention only one point – some of the most prominent Christian nations are heavily implicated in racialism, and a religion that cannot deal with racialism among its own members is unlikely to be able to offer much to the solution of other world problems. Each religion has advantages and disadvantages as it faces the tasks ahead. Among the advantages of Islam are its achievement of brotherhood and its depth of conviction. The self-confidence associated with deep conviction, however, is a disadvantage when it blinds a man to what is good in others; and Islam may find it difficult to incorporate the values of other religions. Islam is certainly a strong contender for the supplying of the basic framework of the one religion of the future.

It is unnecessary, however, at the present date to try to forecast the future more clearly. What precisely happens will not be the result of human planning but will be the work of the forces emerging from the unconscious, or, if one likes, will be the divine overriding of all human plans. While L.S.Thornton would probably not agree with some of the conclusions of this chapter, it may be concluded with a remark of his which, though written about the various strands within Christianity, may also be applied to the different religions of the world:

'. . . the true traditionalist clings, consciously or unconsciously, to an organic conception of truth. Every element in the tradition has *some* truth. It is better, therefore, 'to let both grow together', lest the attempt to make these elements into a harmonious system should destroy something integral to the organic whole which is still in process of growth. There are times when it is the part of wisdom to leave questions undecided until the developing force of truth puts the issue beyond doubt.'[2]

NOTES

ʚ

Chapter One

1. This is the view of Barth as summarized by John Macquarrie, *God-talk: an Examination of the Language and Logic of Theology*, London, 1967.
2. L.S. Thornton, *Revelation and the Modern World*, London, 1950, 194 cf. 60, 'revelation affirms a special divine activity to which there is a specific human response.'
3. Thornton, 226.
4. E.g. Joseph Neuner (ed.), *Christian Revelation and World Religions*, London 1967, with papers by Hans Küng, Piet Fransen, Joseph Masson, R. Panikkar.
5. *Revelation and the Modern World*, 62, etc.

Chapter Two

1. Aṭ-Ṭabarī, *Annales*, i.1147f. cf *Muhammad at Mecca*, Oxford, 1953, 40.
2. Al-Bukhārī, *Ṣaḥīḥ*, i.2; cf. *Muhammad at Mecca*, 55.
3. Cf. 10.15/16 and 69.44-7 which speak of the severe penalties for altering or forging revelations.
4. *Muhammad at Mecca*, 101-9.
5. 10.38/9; 11.13/16.

Chapter Three

1. Cf. Watt, 'The Early Development of the Muslim Attitude to the Bible,' in *Transactions of the Glasgow University Oriental Society*, xvi (1957), 50-62.
2. Cf. *Revelation and the Modern World*, 242, 272.

Chapter Four

1. See esp. 62-85 cf. also *Muhammad Prophet and Statesman*, London, 1961, 22-34.
2. This point is made in *Revelation and the Modern World*, 195, 199.

Chapter Five

1. For the idea of a succession of authoritative teachers in Judaism, cf. *Revelation and the Modern World*, 207, 282.
2. *Islam and the Integration of Society*, London, 1961, ch.4 *Truth in the Religions*, Edinburgh, 1963, ch. 5.

Chapter Six

1. Cf. *Revelation and the Modern World*, 60.
2. Cf. *Islam and Integration*, 139-42, etc.
3. Cf. Watt, 'Khārijite Thought in the Umayyad period', *Der Islam*, xxxvi (1961), 215-31.
4. Cf. al-Ash'arī's principles of exegesis as described by Michel Allard, *Le Problème des attributs divins*, Beirut, 1965, 412, 415.
5. Cf. *Revelation and the Modern World*, 274-91, and index.

Chapter Eight

1. *Revelation and the Modern World*, 13.
2. *Revelation and the Modern World*, 288.
3. *The making of Europe*, London, 1932, 107.
4. The phrase is frequently used in *Revelation and the Modern World* e.g. 4.
5. Cf. *Revelation and the Modern World*, 63; also 65, 273.
6. Cf. *Revelation and the Modern World*, 298.

Chapter Nine

1. Cf. Macquarrie, *God-talk*, 220.
2. The political implications of these doctrines have been mentioned above, pp. 73f.
3. E.g. 12.109 36.15/14.
4. 25.7/8f. cf. 20/2.
5. Cf. *Revelation and the Modern World*, 22: 'true religion . . . is the appointed organ of revelation.'
6. Victor White, *God and the Unconscious*, London, 1960, 203.

Chapter Ten

1. Henri Nusslé, *Dialogue avec l'Islam*, Neuchâtel, 1949, 147.
2. *Revelation and the Modern World*, 293.

INDEX

۩

'*abd*, 13
Abraham
  association with Mecca, 52,
    89, 116
  Christianity and, 8-9, 86,
    87-8, 89
  in the Qur'an, 51-2, 86-90
  Judaism and, 86, 89
  religion of, 8-9, 51-2, 86,
    87-8, 89-90, 100
abrogation, theory of, 18-19, 20
Abū-Bakr, 20-1
Abyssinia, 38, 99
Achan, 49-50
Adam, 35
agricultural life, 25-6, 40
Ai, 49-50
'Ā'isha, 16
ajal, 32, 36-7
Alexander the Great, 95, 96
angels, 13, 14-15, 16, 26, 38
  103, 107, 108, 109
anthropomorphists, 81-2, 83, 85
anzala, 14-15
Arabic
  conception of knowledge,
    61-8
  language, 25-6, 28
  Qur'an, an, 6, 25-30, 106
Arabs, desert life of, 25, 31, 32-3
Ash'arites, 34
'Āṣim, 23
atomism, 33, 77-8
attributes of God, 104-5
awḥā, 13-14

āya, 35
Azāriqa, 76

Badr, Battle of, 27, 50, 51, 60,
  71, 86
Bell, Richard, 14
Biblical stories, 41-2, 101
bid'a, 33
biographical dictionaries, 64
Black Muslims, 108
blind man, 70
Byzantine Empire, 29, 38, 95, 99

Canaanite religion, 48, 88, 102
  122
categorial
  differences, 67-8, 121
  presuppositions, 30-6, 77,
    106, 112
Christianity
  alignment with Greek
    culture, 96-7, 114
  contact with pre-Islamic
    Arabs, 29, 30, 38
  cosmology, 36, 38
  defences of, 88, 122
  failure of, in Middle East,
    94-8, 99
  historical organism of, 8-11,
    59
  in Roman Empire, 1, 2, 10,
    117-18
  Islam and, 3, 13, 18, 45, 48,
    51-2, 70, 99-100, 102,
    114-17

dialogue
  conception of, 2, 120-1
  conditions needed for, 8,
    121-2
  cultural regions and, 121
  mission and, 117-26
  need for, 115
  with science, 4-5, 116, 126
dīn, 4
disobedience, 49-50
distortions, 88, 112, 122

ectosoma, 9-10, 11, 59, 91
education, 64
Egypt, 1, 28, 94, 95, 96, 98-9, 100
elephant, men of the, 40-1, 50
endosoma, 9, 10, 11, 59, 91, 93,
    94
European civilization, 2, 5,
    67-8
exegesis, 77-8
expansion
  Arab, 91-2
  of Christianity, 9, 27-8
  of Islam, 11, 28, 72, 91-2

forgetting, 19-20
Foucauld, Charles de, 124
Freud, S., 17
'fruits' of religion, 116-17, 123,
    125, 127, 128

Gabriel, 13, 15, 103
generosity, 45-6
al-Ghazālī, 66, 82, 101-2
good and evil, 39
grammar, 30, 31, 69-70, 100-1
Greek
  conception of man, 28, 97
  culture, 29, 92, 95-6, 98, 99,
    114, 117
  philosophy, 28, 38, 95, 98, 99,
    101-2, 115
  science, 38, 95, 98, 101, 115

Ḥafṣ, 23
Ḥafṣa, 21, 23
Hamlet, 29
Ḥanbalites, 34
ḥanīf, 86, 87
Hausa, 28
'high god', 37
ḥikāya, 105
historical
  conceptions, 25, 34
  events and information in
    the Qur'an, 52, 53-4, 61,
    105-6
  organism: community and,
    9, 65; focus of, 102; inter-
    pretation and, 72, 78-9; of
    Christianity, 8-11, 59; of
    Islam, 8, 11, 59, 72, 78-9,
    91-4, 107-8; of Israelite
    religion, 110; of religion
    of Abraham, 87-8, 89-90;
    revelation and, 107-8;
    verbal forms and, 68
  presuppositions, 40-3, 112
historicity, 116
history
  irregularity in, 32-3
  Islamic neglect of secular, 63
  thematic process in, 34, 40,
    71
holy war, 91-2
human
  affairs, 33
  activity, 31-2

Ibn-Mas'ūd, 21, 22
Ibn-Mujāhid, 23
Ibn-Rushd, 125
Ibn-Ṭufayl, 125
Ibn-Zayd, 70
idols, 37, 47, 48, 80, 88, 122
ijāra, 39
'ilm, 62
immanence, 82

kin-group, 25, 39
knowledge
    Arabic conception of, 61-8
    as source of power, 62-3
    as wisdom, 62, 65, 66
    European conception of,
      62-3
    transmission of, 65-6

language
    affinity between man and,
      104
    Arabic, 25-6, 28
    culture and, 25-6, 28
    diagrammatic use of, 82-6
    metaphorical, 77, 80-1, 82,
      83
    problem of religious, 80-2,
      83-4, 85-6
    types of use of, 77, 80-1
Last Judgement, 45-6
legal system, 72-3, 127
life energy, 109, 110, 111-12,
    126, 127
linguistic aspects, 4, 80-2, 104
Little Brothers of Jesus, 124
logical consistency, 30, 34-5

Malay, 28
man
    dualistic conception of 28,
      97, 98
    language and, 104
    monistic conception of, 28,
      97-8
maps, 84-5
Marxism, 11
Maryam, 42, 103
Mecca, 6, 7, 13, 45, 48, 50, 106,
    112
Medina, 46, 48, 51, 106, 112
memorizing, 62, 64, 65
mentality
    Arab, 29-30, 35-6, 115

mentality – *contd.*
    categorial presuppositions of
      30-6
    common Islamic, 28-9, 115
    cultural regions, and, 28-9,
      115
    homogeneous world, 128
    Qur'anic, 17, 28-9, 69
    scientific outlook and, 3, 96,
      108, 114
messenger
    Jesus as, 55
    Muhammad as, 5-6, 7, 45,
      46, 51, 57, 106-7
    word for, 39
metaphors, 77, 80-1, 82, 83
Middle East
    culture, Islam and, 92-3,
      97-8
    failure of Christianity in,
      94-8
mission
    and dialogue, 117-26
    changed conception of, 120,
      124-5
    Christian, 63, 67-8, 117-20,
      124
    Islamic, 11, 119-20
Monophysites, 95, 99
monotheism, 88-9, 98
morality, 45-6
Moses, 59, 60, 103
Muhammad
    as messenger, 5-6, 7, 45, 46,
      51, 57, 106-7
    as warner, 7, 45, 46, 57, 60
    his experience of revelation,
      12-24, 108-9
mukhālafa, 82
al-Mutawakkil, 92
Mu'tazilites, 101

nafs, 98
names, 35, 37